Three-Dimensional Beamforming Training Framework for High-Frequency Wireless Networks

Rashmi P.

Three-Dimensional Beamforming Training Framework for High-Frequency Wireless Networks

First Edition October 2024

Written by Rashmi P.

TABLE OF CONTENTS

CHAPTER 1

Introduction

1.1 MOTIVATION FOR 5G

Mobile communication is undoubtedly one of the breakthrough inventions in recent history and has undergone several evolution stages since the introduction of 1G in the 1980s. Rapid advancements in smartphone technology and computation algorithms prepared the ground for the significant changeover in the actual application of mobile communication. The transition from a short-range wireless network with a limited number of users in 1G to an extensive broadband global mobile communication technology with a very high data rate in 4G happened over 30 years. 4G was released in 2008 and can support up to 1Gbps of data speed. Moreover, 4G facilitated high-quality voice and internet calls with good security and uninterrupted connectivity while providing universal roaming facility. Other features supported by 4G are video conferencing, high-definition mobile TV, 3D TV, and gaming services. Subsequently, with the increased availability and popularity of smartphones and other mobile data devices (iPads, laptops, netbooks, ebook readers, digital media etc.), mobile data traffic has seen exceptional growth. According to the Ericsson Mobile data traffic outlook-2022, the total global mobile network traffic, excluding the traffic generated by fixed wireless access, reached around 67 exabytes per month by the end of 2021 and is projected to grow by a factor of around 4.2 to reach 282 exabytes per month in 2027 (Ericsson, 2022*a*). The network handlers have tried their best to support such enormous data traffic by deploying more base stations and installing large heterogeneous networks along with different modulation schemes. However, the microwave frequency spectrum (also called the sub-6 GHz band) and the bandwidth per network operator in 4G (about 200MHz over all the allocated bands) started getting extremely congested and fragmented (Rappaport *et al.*, 2013).

This spurred the need for the fifth generation (5G) technology with a larger bandwidth to support the exponential growth of traffic volume. 5G was first introduced in 2019, and since then, the subscriptions have grown by 70 million during the first quarter of 2022 and is expected to surpass one billion by the end of this year as predicted in Ericsson surveys (Ericsson, 2022*a*). The downlink peak data rate for 5G as per the International Mobile Telecommunications-2020 standard is 20Gbps, and the latency is 4ms. With the capability to support high peak data rates at very low latency, around 60% of the total mobile network traffic is expected to be handled by 5G's new radio mobile technology (5G-NR) by 2027. Because of the migration to 5G, the subscribers in 4G is estimated to approach a peak value of 5 billion subscribers this year and then fall to around 3.5 billion by the end of 2027 (Ericsson, 2022*b*).

1.2   KEY FEATURES OF 5G

5G, compared with 4G, has better coverage, increased scalability, low latency, high reliability and improved energy efficiency. One of the major adaptations in 5G is the use of millimeter waves along with the existing sub-6GHz spectrum (Xiao *et al.*, 2017; O. E. Ayach, S. Rajagopal, S. Abu-Surra, Z. Pi and R. W. Heath, 2014; Zhang *et al.*, 2014). Millimeter wave frequency band refers to the abundant underutilized and unlicensed extremely high-frequency band of frequencies within 30 to 300 GHz range.

However, in wireless communication, millimeter wave commonly refers to frequencies above 24GHz. Operations in 26, 28, and 39 GHz has been standardized and deployed. There exist various international standards for mmWave communications as of now, some of which are WirelessHD, ECMA-387, IEEE 802.15.3c, WiGig, IEEE 802.11ad, and 3GPP NR (Wang *et al.*, 2018).

In order to study the mmWave characteristics and model the propagation nature, several deployments and prototypes were developed by academia, industries, and network-providing companies (Sun *et al.*, 2017; Jaeckel *et al.*, 2014; Wu *et al.*, 2018). Millimeter wave signals were identified to have large pathloss and blocked by everyday objects (human body, plants, raindrops, etc.), making mmWave communication challenging compared to sub-6GHz communication (Rappaport *et al.*, 2017). Hence, other technologies come into play along with mmWave in 5G.

Key enabling technologies adopted in 5G apart from mmWaves that enable high data traffic are dense small cell networks, heterogeneous networks, massive MIMO, and hybrid beamforming (Akyildiz *et al.*, 2016). Small cell networks contain cells of smaller footprint served by low-power transmitters to accommodate a large number of users. It is difficult to densify traditional macro BSs because of the limitation in space and the high expense associated with BS installation (Hunukumbure *et al.*, 2022; Barb and Otesteanu, 2018). The users can be offloaded from busier cells to cells with lesser traffic and thereby reducing the peak load and chances of signal loss. Flexibility over downlink quality of service can also be attained for specific applications by appropriately setting the cell sizes. Heterogeneous networks, popular as HetNets, consist of many small cells deployed along with macro cells for improved range and connectivity (Hunukumbure *et al.*, 2022). Massive MIMO employs antenna arrays with many antennas to accomplish multi-stream and multi-user communication. The antenna structure also facilitates the generation of narrow beams in mmWave communication, which can realize considerable communication range by appropriate beam steering. The constituting antenna elements can be arranged in one dimension or two dimension. The one-dimensional arrangement forms linear arrays, which allow the formation of directional beams over different azimuth angles. However, to form three-dimensional beams with directivity along both azimuth and elevation directions, two-dimensional array placement is required. The upgradation in the Complementary Metal Oxide Semiconductor (CMOS) technology and advancements in antenna array fabrication techniques (Gutierrez et al., 2009; Hong et al., 2014; Roh et al., 2014) facilitated the fabrication of tightly placed small sized antenna arrays with small form factors for massive MIMO. The hybrid beamforming method is an empowering scheme for MIMO and is a mix of analog and digital beamforming methods, which creates multiple simultaneous narrow beams to realize multi-user communication and faster transmission.

1.3 CHALLENGES AND OBJECTIVES

As mentioned in Section 1.2, directional signaling with narrow beams is crucial in mmWave cellular networks to ensure reliable communication with satisfiable array gain. Cell Discovery (CD) is the initial step of wireless communication by which user equipment (UE) entering the network detects, identifies, and gets linked with a suitable

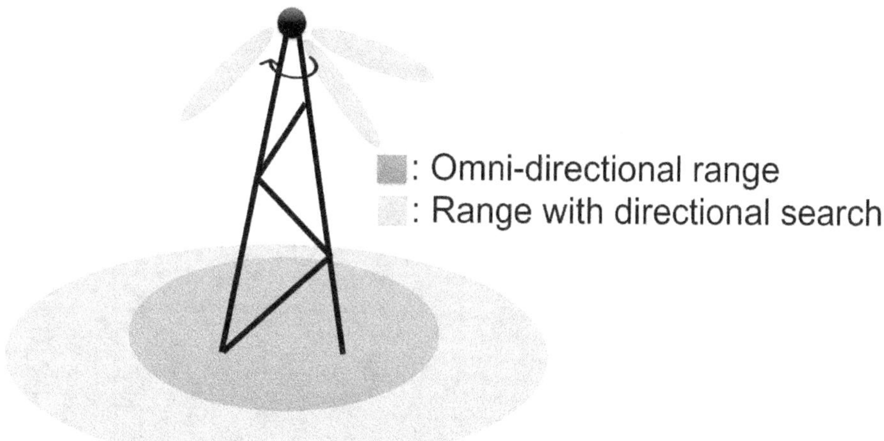

Figure 1.1: Comparison between the transmission range for omnidirectional and directional search

accessible base station (BS) (Rajamohan and Kannu, 2015). Sub-6GHz systems rely on omnidirectional transmission for CD, which is infeasible in mmWave systems due to its significant propagation loss. Hence, in-order to attain reliable communication range, directional beams need to be used. Figure 1.1 illustrates the range achieved by omnidirectional and directional mmWave search schemes. The directional beams concentrate the transmission energy over small angular sectors, thereby, intelligently tackling the propagation loss associated with mmWave systems. On the other hand, blockage is another major issue in mmWave systems because of the smaller operating wavelength. Many BSs will be blocked with respect to the UE in practical scenarios. Hence, the accessible BS need not be the nearest BS as shown in Figure 1.2. In this case, the signals from BS-1 and BS-3 are blocked due to the presence of the building and tree, respectively. Hence, CD involves identifying and finding the corresponding accessible path with BS-2.

However, relying on directional beams poses various challenges in CD. First, directional

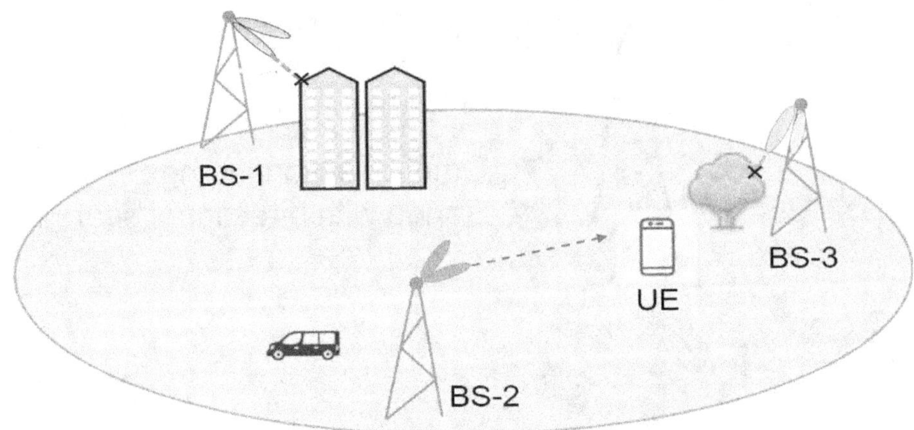

Figure 1.2: Illustration of Cell discovery procedure

beams require the beams to be progressively steered to cover the search space, which introduces additional latency and time overhead. Secondly, CD in mmWave requires signal processing algorithms and hardware architectures that are scalable with the number of antennas and BSs, to support the small cells with large users and MIMO antenna architecture. Finally, UE algorithms associated with CD need to be less complex and fast, so that it can handle the huge volume of data from many BSs simultaneously, within the coherence time. Due to the increased frequency of operation, the coherence time associated with mmWaves is considerably small when compared with that of the sub-6 GHz. Undeniably, CD is a crucial step in mmWave communication and is the first stage of the communication process. Once UE is linked with one or more BSs in the CD step, UE has to estimate the complete mmWave channel of these BSs before the data transfer phase. The channel estimation for mmWave systems is hence equally complicated and poses the same challenges as that of CD.

An accurate CD aids the subsequent channel estimation phase, which then determines the quality of data transmission. This thesis dissertation aims at finding a scalable, fast CD scheme for mmWave systems adhering to the specifications of 5G New Radio (5G NR) (Giordani *et al.*, 2019*a*), which provides deterministic construction of beamforming vectors and is realizable with a simple receiver algorithm. The deterministic approach for beamforming vector construction removes the burden of storing large dictionary matrices at the UE. The desirable properties of the designed training beams along with the UE algorithm make it applicable for mmWave systems, and hence we implement the same to solve the channel estimation problem.

1.4 LITERATURE SURVEY ON MMWAVE BEAMFORMING

Numerous works discuss different beamforming training schemes and the associated receiver algorithms for cell discovery. Directional beamforming is first studied in (Barati *et al.*, 2015), and the authors propose a Generalised Likelihood Ratio Testing based detection algorithm for cell discovery. The authors concluded that directional beams are essential in mmWave systems for a better achievable range. The conventional straightforward approach for CD is the Beam sweeping scheme (Rashmi *et al.*, 2022; Barati *et al.*, 2016; Hur *et al.*, 2013), where both transmitter and receiver sweep their beams along the entire angular range (say, 360 degrees) and make a detection based on the angle of arrival (AoA) - angle of departure (AoD) beam-pair corresponding to the largest received signal strength. In general, beam sweeping incurs significant training overhead, as all the beam-pair combinations must be tried before making a decision. Channel estimation by sweeping over quantised spatial angles by selecting columns of Discrete Fourier Transform matrix (DFT) as training beamforming vectors have been discussed in (Ye *et al.*, 2019; Chung and Kim, 2022). Beamtracking for both slow and fast varying channels using DFT training beams and a Maximum Aposteriory Probability (MAP) based receiver algorithm is addressed in (Zhang *et al.*, 2019).

In order to reduce the overhead of beam sweep, several variations have been proposed in the literature. In the work in (Barati *et al.*, 2015), a detection algorithm with omnidirectional transmission and directed reception is shown to have a better tradeoff over the directional beam sweep in terms of received signal-to-noise ratio (SNR) versus detection delay. Beamforming using broadened beams was proposed in (Raghavan *et al.*, 2016) and is verified to be superior to the traditional multiple signal classification (MUSIC) and Estimation of Signal Parameters Via Rotational Invariance Techniques (ESPRIT) algorithms, which are commonly employed for AoA estimation in wireless communication. A variation by randomly combining the columns of DFT vectors for beam allignment is proposed in (Khordad *et al.*, 2019). However, omnidirectional and widened beams always impose a tradeoff between the achievable channel path resolution and the training overhead. A more generalized version using multi-finger beams in the angle domain for mmWave beam alignment is discussed in (Song *et al.*, 2019), where the Non-Negative Least Squares technique is used to find the strongest path for each UE efficiently. The authors considered both slow and fast varying channels and showed the superior performance of their scheme. However, the extension to a practical scenario with multiple BS is quite non-trivial. Further, the receiver algorithm complexity, being a convex optimization problem, scales with the number of BSs.

Another approach for cell discovery is by using iterative search algorithms (Giordani *et al.*, 2016; Cheng *et al.*, 2022) using feedback. The BS and UE scan its space sector-wise (or omnidirectional transmission), and when the BS speculates the existence of the UE in a particular sector via feedback, it partitions the identified sector into smaller sectors and scans them using narrower beams iteratively. In (Habib *et al.*, 2017), a hybrid cell search method is proposed, which combines the critical aspects of the exhaustive search and the iterative search techniques. Sector-based sequential scanning strategy is proposed in (Soleimani *et al.*, 2018) and (Parada and Zorzi, 2017) in which the order of the search is prioritized based on the time statistics and the entrance statistics of the UEs. While the complexity of the technique remains the same as the iterative search mechanism, the approach significantly improves the delay in the CD if the required statistical environment is known/learned well at the BS. An Adaptive hierarchical beam training scheme is discussed in (Zhang *et al.*, 2020*a*) where the training time is adaptively updated to achieve reduced training overhead. A 3D peak-finding algorithm is proposed in (Aykin and Krunz, 2020), in which the transmit beamforming vectors are iteratively selected following the direction of increased received signal energy by using feedback. In (Hussain and Michelusi, 2018), an interactive energy-efficient beam-alignment protocol is developed that optimizes the sequence of beams used for training and the duration of the beam-alignment procedure. The updated beamforming vectors are designed/selected in hierarchical and iterative search schemes based on feedback from the user end, which establishes the training duration and the cell detection rate. However, all these iterative schemes rely on the feedback/location information of the UE to refine the beams. This introduces immense delay for beamforming in mmWave networks with many users.

An approach that is very much similar to iterative beam search is by using multiresolution beamforming codebooks (Noh *et al.*, 2017). In (Noh *et al.*, 2017), the codebook is designed to adaptively maximize the average rate to quickly enable the system to search out the dominant channel direction for single-path channels. The resulting design gives a well-balanced codebook that minimizes the training overhead and maximizes the beamforming gain. Even though the technique can be extended to multipath mmWave channels, the complexity scales with the increase in the number of paths. Also, the authors do not discuss applying the same when multiple BSs are present in the network. An iterative search algorithm was implemented in IEEE 802.11ad (Nitsche *et al.*, 2014) where BS do exhaustive search using narrow beams while the UE listens in the omnidirectional mode. In the next cycle, UE keeps the beam fixed while BS searches for the possible beam match.

Exploiting the sparse nature of mmWave channels, pseudo-random beams are used for beam training in (Han and Danijela, 2019; Alkhateeb *et al.*, 2015; Manoj and Kannu, 2018; Wang *et al.*, 2016). The training scheme (termed as 'Random Beamforming (RBF)') uses beamforming vectors with scaled random $\pm 1 \pm j$ entries (Han and Danijela, 2019) and provides flexibility over the number of beamforming vectors to be used. (Alkhateeb *et al.*, 2015) and (Wang *et al.*, 2016) uses unit magnitude entries with random phase, while (Manoj and Kannu, 2018) uses random Bernoulli ± 1 entries in the beamforming vector. However, all the above schemes require the randomly generated beamforming vectors to be stored at the BSs and UEs, which can be prohibitively large in networks with high BS and UE density. The authors of (Yan and Liu, 2018) proposed to use multiple beams leveraging multiple RF chains for beam search. In this work, orthogonal pilots are transmitted over each RF chain inorder to facilitate BS identification at the UE.

CD schemes using context information is proposed in (Filippini *et al.*, 2018; Devoti *et al.*, 2016; Rezagah *et al.*, 2015; Alexandropoulos, 2017), considering an environment with mmWave pico-cells assisted by a macro BS. More recently, authors of (Sim *et al.*, 2020) proposed a sub-6GHz assisted CD to reduce beam sweeping overhead, in which the power delay profile (PDP) of the sub-6GHz system is estimated using a Third Generation Partnership Project (3GPP)-New Radio (NR) based channel state information acquisition technique and Deep learning based beam selection is used at the BS in order to reduce the search space. However, the performance of these schemes completely relies on the availability and accuracy of the estimate on user position/channel PDP. (Guo *et al.*, 2018) and (V. D. P. Souto *et al.*, 2019) propose beamforming codebook optimization using a genetic algorithm for the initial access problem. The setup in (Guo *et al.*, 2018) consists of a single transmitter and multiple vehicular UE receptors but assumes complete channel state information at the UEs. Even though the work in (V. D. P. Souto *et al.*, 2019) does not require Channel State Information (CSI), the algorithm is developed only for a single transmitter single receiver scenario. Enhancements for the non-standalone NR plus Long-Term Evolution-E-UTRAN New Radio-Dual Connectivity (LTE ENDC) network architecture were proposed in (Giordani *et al.*, 2019*b*) to reduce the latency of CD and improve reactivity for radio link failure scenarios in the conventional beam management scheme that is included in the 3GPP-NR standards. The authors concluded that a non-standalone architecture could guarantee a better end-to-end performance through simulations.

Alternative approach to cell discovery is based on estimating the partial or complete channel information at the UE (Saeid and Giuseppe, 2016). Traditional channel estimation methods like Least Square (LS) and Minimum Mean Squared Error (MMSE) estimators cannot be applied for MIMO systems because of the requirement of large matrix inversion operations. Further, these operators do not take advantage of the sparse nature of the mmWave channel and hence, output erroneous estimates (Shukla et al., 2022). The channel estimation schemes can be broadly classified into two, namely, open loop and closed loop methods. In general, the compressive sensing and Sparse Bayesian Learning (SBL) based channel estimation methods are open-loop schemes. There are many channel estimation schemes based on compressive sensing methodology (Manoj and Kannu, 2018; Wang et al., 2016). The authors of (Sethi and Raja Kumar, 2020) propose an approximate conjugate gradient pursuit algorithm that attains the same performance as the Orthogonal Matching Pursuit (OMP) algorithm but with less complexity. In (Wu et al., 2022), the authors decomposed the hybrid channel estimation framework to elevation angle and azimuth angle estimation problems. Compressive sensing-based estimation is done in the elevation domain, and an SBL-based estimation is used in the azimuth domain. Other bayesian channel estimation methods include using bayesian matching pursuit, expectation-maximization algorithm, and bayesian compressive sensing. (You and Zhang, 2020; Rodríguez-Fernández, 2022). The bayesian approach makes appropriate statistics assumptions and finds solutions to minimize the posterior estimation error. Closed loop channel estimation schemes update the training beams iteratively based on the feedback from the UE (Xiao et al., 2019; Sun and Rappaport, 2017; Robaei et al., 2022). Apart from the feedback overhead, closed-loop systems tend to perform badly in outdoor scenarios because of the power limitations in using wider beams.

Another method for channel estimation using atomic norm minimization is discussed in (Li *et al.*, 2022*a*). The second-order channel statistics are estimated at the UE using repeated channel probing and UE-based uplink training in (Song *et al.*, 2018; Shukla *et al.*, 2022) to leverage beamforming training for fast varying fast mmWave channels. In general, CD schemes based on partial/complete channel estimation require sophisticated receiver algorithms, and the complexity of such algorithms scales with the number of BSs and the antenna dimensions. However, the channel estimation step comes after cell discovery phase and the UE would have already decided on the subset of BSs to communicate at this point. Thus, the receiver algorithm for channel estimation can be more rigorous than the one used for cell discovery problem, owing towards better estimation.

Recently, there are many works that consider the practical aspects of mmWave systems. In (Lim *et al.*, 2020; Robaei and Akl, 2020; Chavva and Mehta, 2021), the authors consider the user mobility and spatial consistency of mmWave channels for channel estimation. Channel estimation with 1-bit Analog to Digital Converter (ADC) at the receiver is studied in (Zhou *et al.*, 2022; Myers *et al.*, 2020). Non linear receiver structures based on approximate message passing algorithms are proposed for channel estimation in (Li *et al.*, 2022*b*; Thomas *et al.*, 2021). The hardware impairements related to a tranceiver setting with hybrid beamforming architecture is studied in (Maletic *et al.*, 2020).

Machine learning and deep learning-based initial access methods are discussed in (Wang *et al.*, 2022; Ma *et al.*, 2020; Yan *et al.*, 2020) when CD is done with one BS in the network. As mentioned in (Wang *et al.*, 2022), the complexity of the receiver algorithm will be higher than the other beam sweeping algorithms. Works in (Wang *et al.*, 2022) and (Ma *et al.*, 2020) do not discuss CD when multiple BSs are present in the network, and a direct extension to multiple BS environments will significantly increase the receiver complexity. Machine learning, deep learning and neural network based mmWave channel estimation is discussed in (Zhang *et al.*, 2020b; Wei *et al.*, 2021; Thomas *et al.*, 2021)

1.5 SCOPE AND CONTRIBUTIONS

In view of the above works, in this thesis, we address the CD problem in mmWave systems. We aim to develop beamforming vectors that can identify the correct AoA-AoD alignment between the BS and UE without using any feedback during the CD procedure. We focus on mmWave networks with multiple BSs in which the UE try to detect and identify an accessible BS with fewer measurements and a less complex UE algorithm. We consider two-dimensional and three-dimensional beamforming using unform linear and uniform planar antennas, respectively. The main contributions of this thesis are summarised below:

- To invoke the importance of a compressive sensing-based training scheme, we first elaborately discuss the most popular and extensively used conventional beam sweeping scheme (CBS) and beam combining (BC) schemes to solve cell discovery problems. In this method, the transmitter and receiver exhaustively search the optimal AoA-AoD pair by sweeping their beams in the entire $[0, 2\pi]$ space and using all the transmit/receive beam combinations. The training beamforming vectors are selected as a linear combination of columns of unitary

DFT matrices for the schemes discussed in this work. The beamforming vectors for the BC method realize widened training beams that can achieve faster CD.

We analyze and derive analytical expressions/bounds for the detection probability and false alarm probability for the CBS and BC methods under certain assumptions on the mmWave channel models. We also characterize the time delay associated with CD and the average number of repeated attempts required for CD mathematically and derive analytical expressions for the same under special channel conditions. We also discuss the beam sweeping scheme for multiple BS scenarios using sequence-based transmission and characterize the detection and false alarm probability when BSs use orthogonal sequences during training. To the best of our knowledge, such analysis does not exist for CBS and BC schemes.

- By exploiting the sparse nature of mmWave channels, we formulate CD as a sparse signal recovery problem in compressive sensing (CS) and develop a new training scheme in which the beamforming vectors are designed based on mutually unbiased bases (MUB) from quantum information theory (Li and Ge, 2014). We explicitly define the beamforming vectors to be used for MUB based training scheme (MUBB) and derive the mutual coherence[1] parameter of the constructed sensing matrix for both linear and planar antenna arrays. The mutual coherence parameter depends on the beamforming vectors used at the BSs and UEs, and indirectly determines the BS identification capability of UE. Our proposed construction provides a deterministic easy way of finding beamforming vectors for BSs and guarantees good (the smaller the mutual coherence, the better the detection at the UE) mutual coherence which in turn helps the BS identification at the UE. In coherence with the constructed sensing matrix, we propose a receiver algorithm of lesser complexity. The developed MUBB approach opens up a simple, deterministic, and scalable way of constructing beamforming vectors for CD and can be an easy replacement for the quite extensively used random beamforming (RBF) scheme.

We obtain analytical expressions for the lower bound of the detection probability and false alarm probability for the generalized compressive sensing-based cell discovery problem. Using the same, we evaluate the bound on the analytical probability of detection and false alarm for MUBB, and relate it with the mutual coherence of the sensing matrix obtained in the compressive sensing-based system model. We show that the sensing matrix is only a function of the beamforming vectors, establishing that properly designed beamforming vectors can lead to higher detection probability.

Owing to faster cell discovery, we propose MUB based training scheme using coarser beams (MUBB$^{(w)}$) in order to accomplish CD with a smaller number of beams by sensing the mmWave channel at lesser resolution. By tuning the resolution parameter, the beam width of MUBB$^{(w)}$ can be varied according to the user/application requirement. Further, we characterize the mutual coherence of the MUBB$^{(w)}$ method in terms of the resolution parameter.

---

[1]Mutual coherence of a matrix characterizes the maximum correlation between any two columns of a matrix.

- We discuss how the CD schemes can be extended to the more generic mmWave hybrid beamforming architecture for both linear and planar antenna arrays. With a hybrid beamforming architecture, multi-stream transmission can be supported using multiple radio frequency (RF) chains for nominal costs. With multiple RF chains at the receiver, multiple received observations can be obtained in a single instance using different receive beamforming vectors, requiring fewer transmissions.

- We propose a search space-aware MUB-based training scheme to incorporate apriori search space restrictions known at the BS and UE while designing beamforming vectors for CD. For example, when BS/UE is mounted on (near to) a wall or when sector-based antennas are used, the directional transmissions can be confined to a particular angular sector. With the reduction in the intended search space, we show that the number of beamforming vectors for MUB based training scheme can be reduced and hence achieve faster cell discovery. We prove that the guarantees of mutual coherence can be extended for the search space reduction condition. We also explain in detail how our proposed scheme is in complete agreement with the 5G NR framework for cell discovery.

- Finally, we present detailed simulation results and establish the superior performance of our MUBB method over the conventional beam combining (CBS, BC) and the random beamforming (RBF) schemes in terms of key performance metrics like the probability of detecting BS and post beamforming SNR through simulation studies. We also present detailed simulations based on the practical mmWave channels generated using NYUSIM.

- We extend our developed MUBB based training schemes to solve cell discovery in wideband millimeter wave systems. Through simulations, we substantiate the advantage of using our schemes for better detection of BSs without compromising on the attainable post beamforming SNR.

- Owing to the large number of distinct beamforming vectors realizable using MUB based scheme, we also study the cell discovery performance when no BS-specific transmission sequence is sent to the UE. In this case, cell discovery and the UE algorithm completely depends on the distinctness of the beamforming vectors used by the BSs. Through simulations, we verify the better performance of MUB based training method over the other CD methods.

- We illustrate the relevance and suitability of the proposed schemes with a UE algorithm based on Generalised Block OMP (GBOMP) that exploits the block sparse nature of the mmWave channels. We confirm the performance improvement with MUBB in terms of the probability of detecting atleast one BS and thereby validate the applicability of the developed schemes to different UE algorithms that depend on the mutual coherence of the sensing matrix.

- Through simulations, we show the applicability of MUB vectors for signaling, which can support many BSs with shorter-length sequences.

- We extend the use of MUB-based beamforming vectors for mmWave channel estimation without feedback, and study the performance in the practical channel setup using channels generated using NYUSIM simulator. We consider both 2D and 3D beamforming methods using hybrid beamforming architecture. The simulations are done for two compressive sensing based receiver algorithms, namely, OMP and GBOMP. Our simulation results show that the MUBB method can provide better spectral efficiency and beamforming gain with lesser training overhead.

1.6 THESIS OVERVIEW

In Chapter 2, we explain the mmWave system model for different beamforming architectures and antenna types. We also discuss the mmWave channel formulation and the reasons for channel sparsity. We invoke the idea of accessible multipath between BS and UE from the channel perspective and the importance of beam scanning. In Chapter 3, we present the mathematical formulation for CD problem and discuss the physical layer implementation of the Conventional Beam Sweeping scheme for CD. We model the beam combining scheme to attain faster cell search and analytically characterize the detection performance when an energy detector is used at the UE. In Chapter 4, by exploiting the sparse nature, we propose new training schemes compatible with 5G NR framework based on MUB vectors, providing better detection and deterministic construction possibilities than the training using random beams and beam sweeping schemes. We characterize the probability of detection of at least one base station for a generic model and derive the mutual coherence value for MUB based construction. We also do detailed simulations to show the superior performance of our proposed training scheme. We also explain how to extend the developed scheme to address CD in wideband systems and with other UE algorithms. Motivated by the similarity in the problem formulation and the advantages of the developed MUB-based training schemes, we apply the same to solve the channel estimation problem in Chapter 5. We

also do simulations based on practical channels generated using NYUSIM to validate

this. Finally, we conclude the thesis in Chapter 6 and highlight the future scopes.

CHAPTER 2

Millimeter wave system and channel model

A deep understanding of the mmWave system and channel model, along with the distinct characteristics of each, is fundamental in developing a good beamforming training scheme for cell discovery and channel estimation in mmWave systems. Cell discovery problem deals with identifying an accessible path to a BS when UE comes to a network. As mentioned in Chapter 1, the omnidirectional CD/channel estimation methods adapted in sub-6GHz systems cannot be extended for mmWave systems due to the significant propagation loss. Thus, beamforming vectors need to be designed with good directional gain using large antenna arrays to realize directional beams. Such beams should then be steered sequentially within the search space to find a reliable BS. The underlying design of beamforming vectors depends on two main factors: the antenna type and the beamforming configuration. There are several antenna options like linear antenna array, rectangular antenna array, and lens antenna array for mmWave systems (Heath *et al.*, 2016). Out of the digital, hybrid, and analog beamforming structures, hybrid beamforming can support multi-stream transmission and is the most cost-effective approach with a limited number of RF chains (O. E. Ayach, S. Rajagopal, S. Abu-Surra, Z. Pi and R. W. Heath, 2014). In this chapter, we will first discuss the system model for the CD problem in detail. We then discuss the beamforming vector formulation for the two most common antenna types, particularly Uniform Linear Arrays(ULA) and Uniform Planar Arrays (UPA), for two-dimensional and three-dimensional beam steering. We will also review the hybrid beamforming structure in detail. Then, we explain the mmWave channel model and the reasons for the sparsity of the same. We end the chapter with the sparse formulation of the channel and invoke the idea of the accessible path between a BS and UE from the channel perspective.

2.1 SYSTEM MODEL

Consider a downlink narrowband mmWave network with N_B base stations (BSs), each equipped with an antenna of size N_t. Let the user equipment (UE) has an antenna of size N_r. The presence of blockage/outage/shadowing is a key difference in mmWave systems when compared with conventional sub-6 GHz systems in which each link between BS and UE is classified as either Line of Sight (LoS) or Non-Line of Sight (NLoS). In mmWave networks, each link between BS and UE can be categorized as either LoS, NLoS, or outage. The outage can be due to environmental obstructions and can even occlude all paths (either via reflections or scattering) to the receiver. Henceforth, as discussed in (Akdeniz *et al.*, 2014), we model the channel matrices between blocked BS and UE as zero, and UE receives signal only from a subset $\mathcal{A} \subset \{1, \cdots, N_B\}$ of BSs. Now, consider the training phase where BSs and UE use a fixed set of beamforming vectors and transmit a known set of symbols. That is, UE has a set of P beamforming vectors, $\{\mathbf{w}_r^{(1)}, \cdots, \mathbf{w}_r^{(P)}\}$, each of length N_r. Each of the ith BS uses a set of Q beamforming vectors, $\{\mathbf{w}_{t_i}^{(1)}, \cdots, \mathbf{w}_{t_i}^{(Q)}\}$ of length N_t, and periodically transmits a unique synchronization signal to the UE. Suppose, the ith BS transmits the mth data symbol of its synchronisation signal, $x_{p,q,m}^{(i)}$, to the UE. The received observation corresponding to a given receive/transmit beamforming vector pair, indexed as (p, q), will be ,

$$y_{p,q,m} = \mathbf{w}_r^{(p)*} \sum_{i \in \mathcal{A}} \sqrt{\rho_i} \mathbf{H}_i \mathbf{w}_{t_i}^{(q)} x_{p,q,m}^{(i)} + \underbrace{\mathbf{w}_r^{(p)*} \mathbf{n}_{p,q,m}}_{n_{p.q,m}} . \tag{2.1}$$

Here ρ_i characterizes the transmit power of ith BS, and $\mathbf{n}_{p,q,m}$ is the additive noise vector. $\mathbf{H}_i$ is the channel between i^{th} BS and UE. Throughout this work, we use unit energy data symbols, $x_{p,q,m}^{(i)}, \forall (p,q,i)$. We assume, $\mathbf{n}_{p,q,m} \sim \mathcal{CN}(0, \sigma_n^2 \mathbf{I}_{N_r})$ and hence $n_{p,q,m} \sim \mathcal{CN}(0, \sigma_n^2 ||\mathbf{w}_r^{(p)}||_2^2)$. For convenience and consistency, we assume the beamforming vectors at both BS and UE to be of unit norm, which yields $n_{p,q,m} \sim \mathcal{CN}(0, \sigma_n^2)$.

2.2 ANTENNA STRUCTURE

The beamforming vectors given in (2.1) must be selected according to the type of antenna used. The antenna elements are arranged with equal spacing along a line in ULA, and the directed beams can be steered along the direction perpendicular to the placement of the ULA. Hence, ULA supports only two-dimensional tracking of beams. With many antennas in mmWave systems, UPAs are preferred over ULAs because of their compact arrangement in a rectangular pattern. UPA generates beams with lesser sidelobes compared to ULA and allows beam steering along both azimuth and elevation direction (Balanis, 2015; Van Trees, Harry L, 2004). That is, the beams can be designed to point to any particular angular region in the space.

In this work, we use ULAs of dimension N_t at the BS and N_r at the UE. For UPAs, we set $N_t = N_{t_1} \times N_{t_2}$, with N_{t_1} antennas along the horizontal direction and N_{t_2} antennas along the vertical direction. Hence, N_{t_1} decides the angular resolution along the azimuth direction, and N_{t_2} decides the angular resolution along the elevation direction. Similarly, at receiver, N_{r_1} and N_{r_2} antennas are arranged along the azimuth and elevation directions, respectively, and $N_r = N_{r_1} \times N_{r_2}$. Figure 2.1 shows the

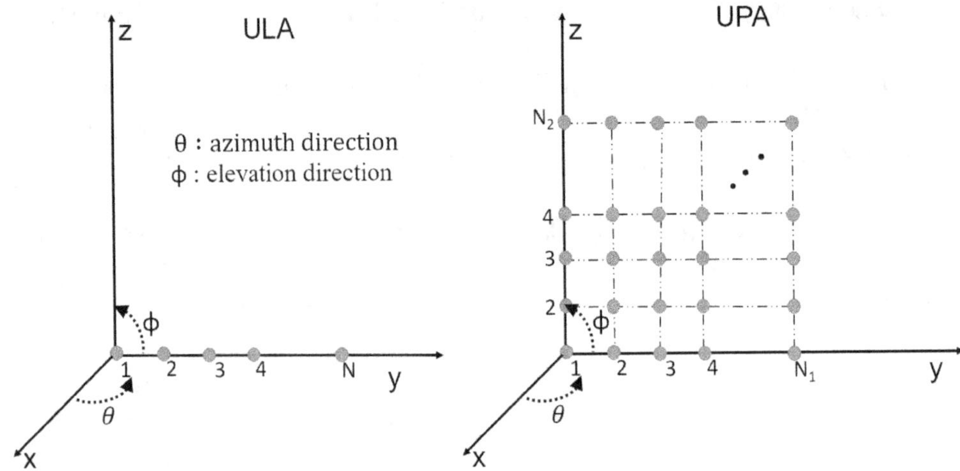

Figure 2.1: ULA along Y axis and UPA along Y-Z direction

schematic for both ULA and UPA.

2.3 BEAMFORMING ARCHITECTURE

Millimeter wave systems require large antenna arrays to achieve good directional gain and received signal strength. The size of the antenna arrays introduces certain hardware constraints in applying the precoding and combining schemes used in sub-6GHz systems for mmWave systems. Based on whether the signal processing happens in analog/digital domain, the beamforming architecture is broadly classified into three types, namely, digital, analog and hybrid schemes.

All the signal processing happens in the digital domain (or base-band) in the fully digital beamforming architecture used in conventional microwave systems. Each antenna element has a dedicated RF chain along with digital to analog converter, analog to digital converter, low noise amplifier, etc (Hansen, 2011). That is the number of RF chains, N_{rf}, is equal to N_t in Figure 2.2. This means that the gain and the phase of the signal at each antenna element can be set independently. Thus digital beamforming architecture allows algorithm implementation with maximum flexibility. Multi-stream transmission is possible with digital beamforming and hence can support multi-beam and multi-user transmissions. However, the hardware constraints cause prohibitive implementation costs and large power consumption for digital architecture.

Analog beamforming was proposed later to realize a simple hardware-efficient transceiver with one RF chain to reduce the implementation cost and power requirement. The restriction to a single RF chain hinders the multi-stream transmission and hence analog beamforming is mainly used in indoor mmWave communication systems only. Further, the signal processing in the RF domain limits the sample values at each antenna to have a unit norm and thereby restricting the beamforming vector design.

Hybrid beamforming allows both multi-stream transmission and flexibility over the unit modulus constraint on the sample entries unlike analog beamforming and can be realized with much lesser hardware cost and power expenditure when compared with digital beamforming. Hence, hybrid beamforming architecture is considered the most promising architecture for mmWave systems recently (O. E. Ayach, S. Rajagopal, S. Abu-Surra, Z. Pi and R. W. Heath, 2014; Lee *et al.*, 2016*b*). In this case, the number of RF chains is greater than 1 and less than the number of antenna elements.

Figure 2.2 shows the block diagram of a MIMO Hybrid beamforming architecture at the UE. The RF chains along with Analog to Digital Converter (ADC) convert the analog RF signal to digital signal. The RF unit is also called an analog beamformer/precoder

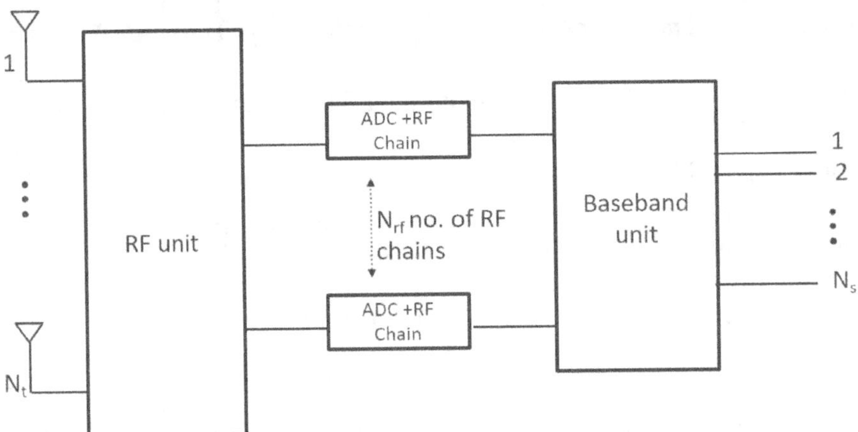

Figure 2.2: Block diagram of hybrid beamforming architecture at the UE

and basically consists of analog phase shifter circuits. The baseband unit or digital

precoder processes the digital data from the RF chain section and appropriately maps

to N_s data streams. Hybrid beamforming structure is of two types based on how the RF

chains are connected to the antennas, namely, fully connected and partially connected

structures. In our work, we assume a fully connected hybrid beamforming architecture,

in which the RF chains have access to the symbols coming from all the antennas. For

partially connected architecture, the symbols from a subset of antennas are only passed

to each RF chain. The implementation of the hybrid beamforming structure at the

transmitter can be done similarly.

With multiple RF chains at the receiver, we can get multiple received observations in

a single time instant by using different receive beamforming vectors (O. E. Ayach, S.

Rajagopal, S. Abu-Surra, Z. Pi and R. W. Heath, 2014; Lee *et al.*, 2016*b*). Suppose

$\mathbf{w}_r^{(p,s)}$ is the receive beamforming vector used at the UE for the sth RF chain, then the measurement obtained is given by,

$$y_{p,q,m}^{(s)} = \mathbf{w}_r^{(p,s)*} \left(\sum_{i \in A} \sqrt{\rho_i} \mathbf{H}_i \mathbf{w}_{t_i}^{(q)} x_{p,q,m}^{(i)} \right) + \underbrace{\mathbf{w}_r^{(p,s)*} \mathbf{n}_{p,q,m}}_{n_{p,q,m}^{(s)}}, \tag{2.2}$$

where $s \in \{1, 2, ..., N_{\text{rf}}\}$ and N_{rf} is the number of RF chains at the UE. At a given

instant, we can get measurements corresponding to N_{rf} receive beams by using N_{rf}

receive RF chains. Hence the duration of the training phase decreases by a factor of N_{rf}.

Essentially, the number of transmissions required to exhaust all the pairs of P receive

and Q transmit beamforming weights will be $M = \frac{PQ}{N_{\text{rf}}}$. If the receive beamforming

vectors at different RF chains $\{\mathbf{w}_r^{(p,s)}, \ s = 1, \cdots, N_{\text{rf}}\}$ at a particular instant (p, q)

can be chosen as orthonormal, it can be shown that the noise samples $n_{p,q,m}^{(s)}$ are i.i.d.

Gaussian.

2.4 CHANNEL MODEL

Based on the extended Saleh-Valenzuela model, the channel from the ith BS to the

UE, denoted by $\mathbf{H}_i$ (of size $N_r \times N_t$), is modelled as (O. E. Ayach, S. Rajagopal, S.

Abu-Surra, Z. Pi and R. W. Heath, 2014; Han and Danijela, 2019),

$$\mathbf{H}_i = \sum_{k=1}^{K_i} \alpha_k^{(i)} \mathbf{a}_{r_k}^{(i)}(\theta_k^r, \phi_k^r) \mathbf{a}_{t_k}^{(i)}(\theta_k^t, \phi_k^t)^*, \tag{2.3}$$

where K_i is the total number of scattering multipath components between UE and i^{th}

BS. $\alpha_k^{(i)}$ is the complex channel gain of the kth path. The authors of (Akdeniz *et al.*,

2014) use real-world measurements in New York City and claim that the complex

channel gains can be modeled using complex Gaussian random variables. Hence, we model $\alpha_k^{(i)}$ as independent random variables distributed as $\mathcal{CN}(0, \sigma_k^{(i)2})$ (Lee *et al.*, 2016*a,b*). $\mathbf{a}_{t_k}^{(i)}$ and $\mathbf{a}_{r_k}^{(i)}$ are the corresponding normalized transmit and receive antenna array response vectors with azimuth (elevation) angles as $\theta_k^t(\phi_k^t)$ and $\theta_k^r(\phi_k^t)$ respectively The AoAs and AoDs can take any arbitrary value between 0 and 2π.

The antenna array response vectors depend on the antenna array structure and can be written as functions of the AoAs and AoDs of the associated multi-paths.

- Case 1: Antenna response vectors for ULA
  The antenna response vectors at the UE and the BS are as given below (O. E. Ayach, S. Rajagopal, S. Abu-Surra, Z. Pi and R. W. Heath, 2014; Lee *et al.*, 2016*b*; Manoj and Kannu, 2018):

$$\mathbf{a}_{r_k} = \frac{1}{\sqrt{N_r}}[1 \; e^{-j\omega_{r_k}} \; \ldots \; e^{-j(N_r-1)\omega_{r_k}}]^T,$$

$$\mathbf{a}_{t_k} = \frac{1}{\sqrt{N_t}}[1 \; e^{-j\omega_{t_k}} \; \ldots \; e^{-j(N_t-1)\omega_{t_k}}]^T.$$

Here $\omega_{r_k} = 2\pi\frac{d}{\lambda}\sin(\theta_k^r)$ and $\omega_{t_k} = 2\pi\frac{d}{\lambda}\sin(\theta_k^t)$. d is the inter-element spacing between adjacent antennas in the ULA (at both the BSs and the UE), λ is the operating carrier wavelength, and θ_k^r and θ_k^t are the AoA and AoD respectively, associated with the kth multi-path component of the channel $\mathbf{H}_i$.

- Case 2: Antenna response vectors for UPA
  For UPA, the antenna response vector at the receiver is given as

$$\mathbf{a}_{r_k}(\theta_k^r, \phi_k^r) = \mathbf{a}^{(az)}(\theta_k^r, \phi_k^r, N_{r_1}) \otimes \mathbf{a}^{(el)}(\phi_k^r, N_{r_2}).$$

$\mathbf{a}^{(el)}(.)$ and $\mathbf{a}^{(az)}(.)$ denotes the constituting smaller antenna response vectors along the elevation and azimuth directions respectively with $\mathbf{a}^{(el)}(\phi, N_2) = \frac{1}{\sqrt{N_2}}[1 \; e^{j\omega n_2 \cos(\phi)} \; \ldots \; e^{j\omega(N_2-1)\cos(\phi)}]$ and $\mathbf{a}^{(az)}(\theta, \phi, N_1) = \frac{1}{\sqrt{N_1}}[1 \; e^{j\omega n_1 \sin(\phi)\sin(\theta)} \; \ldots \; e^{j\omega(N_1-1)\sin(\phi)\sin(\theta)}]$. Here, $\omega = 2\pi\frac{d}{\lambda}$ where d is the inter-element spacing between adjacent antennas in the UPA (at both the BSs and the UE) and is usually set as $\frac{\lambda}{2}$ (S. Jiho and David, 2017). λ is the operating carrier wavelength. The antenna response vector at the BS is defined similarly as $\mathbf{a}_{t_k}(\theta_k^t, \phi_k^t) = \mathbf{a}^{(az)}(\theta_k^t, \phi_k^t, N_{t_1}) \otimes \mathbf{a}^{(el)}(\phi_k^t, N_{t_2})$.

Typically, the number of paths K_i for mmWave channels is very small (The average number of paths at 28GHz is 2.5 as mentioned in Table 3.13 of chapter 3 in

(Rappaport *et al.*, 2015).) when compared with the dimensions of the channel matrix. Each elevation AoA-AoD pair of a path leads to a spatial frequency pair $\left(\omega\cos(\phi_k^r), (\omega\cos(\phi_k^t)\right)$ in the antenna response vector. Similarly, an azimuth AoA-AoD pair contributes to the spatial frequency $\left(\omega\sin(\phi_k^r)\sin(\theta_k^r)\right), \omega\sin(\phi_k^t)\sin(\theta_k^t))$. Hence, when projected onto the columns of the DFT matrix by taking 2D Fourier transformation of $\mathbf{H}_i$, the channel paths will be reflected as signal peaks at the quantized AoA-AoD values in the transformed matrix, $\mathbf{G}_i$. That is,

$$\mathbf{G}_i = \bar{\mathbf{F}}_{N_r}^* \mathbf{H}_i \bar{\mathbf{F}}_{N_t},\tag{2.4}$$

where $\bar{\mathbf{F}}_{N_r} = \mathbf{F}_{N_{r_1}} \otimes \mathbf{F}_{N_{r_2}}$ and $\bar{\mathbf{F}}_{N_t} = \mathbf{F}_{N_{t_1}} \otimes \mathbf{F}_{N_{t_2}}$. $\mathbf{G}_i$ matrix will have significant energies in the DFT bins closer to the spatial frequencies due to spectral leakage (Manoj and Kannu, 2018). Thus, the location of the significant entries in $\mathbf{G}_i$ indicates the AoA and AoD of an accessible path. The column locations indicate the AoD and the row locations map to AoA. So, $\mathbf{G}_i$ is popularly called as *beamspace* matrix.

Since the number of multi-paths is small compared to the array sizes, the mmWave channels are approximately block sparse in Fourier basis (Mo *et al.*, 2014; Lee *et al.*, 2016*b*; Manoj and Kannu, 2018). Figure 2.3(a) shows the absolute channel gain values for a normalized beamspace channel matrix for an $N_t = 32 \times 16$, $N_r = 4 \times 2$ mmWave channel generated using the practical NYUSIM channel generator. The figure clearly shows the spectral leakage due to the arbitrary AoA-AoDs associated with the channel paths, and the block sparse nature of the mmWave channels. In the subsequent chapters, we formulate the cell discovery problem as a sparse recovery problem by exploiting this

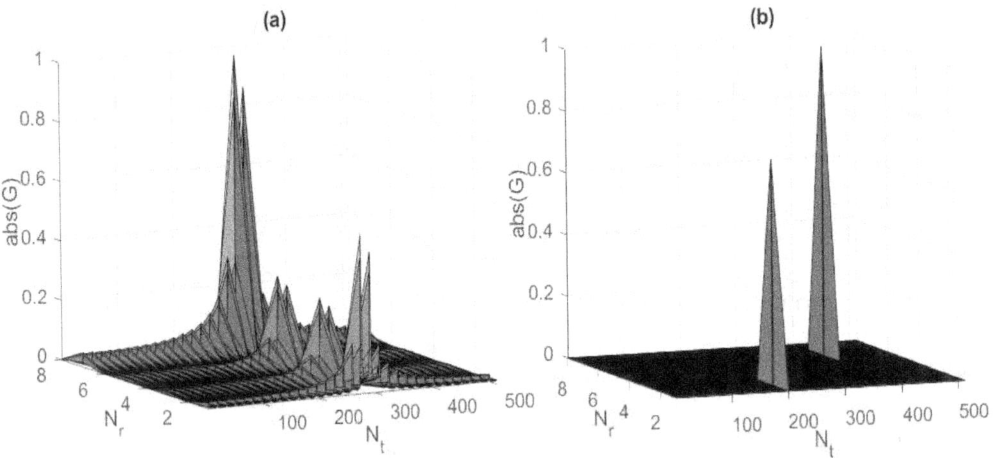

Figure 2.3: (a) Practical beamspace channel (b) Beamspace channel with *on-grid* assumption

beamspace channel structure

2.4.1 Ideal on-grid channel

In the special case when the spatial frequencies fall exactly on the DFT bins, matrix $\mathbf{G}_i$ is *exactly* sparse, then, the spatial frequency corresponding to the elevation and azimuth AoAs of each path belongs to $\left\{ \frac{2\pi l_1}{N_{r_1}}, l_1 = 0, ..., N_{r_1} - 1 \right\}$ and $\left\{ \frac{2\pi l_2}{N_{r_1}}, l_2 = 0, ..., N_{r_2} - 1 \right\}$ respectively. Similarly, spatial frequencies corresponding to elevation and azimuth AoDs of each path belong to $\left\{ \frac{2\pi k_1}{N_{t_1}}, k_1 = 0, ..., N_{t_1} - 1 \right\}$ and $\left\{ \frac{2\pi k_2}{N_{t_1}}, k_2 = 0, ..., N_{t_2} - 1 \right\}$. The entries in the $\mathbf{G}_i$ matrix will be Gaussian non-zero entries in the DFT bins given by the analogous spatial frequency pair. We refer to this special case as the *ideal on-grid channels*.

The beamspace channel matrix for an $N_t = 32 \times 16, N_r = 4 \times 2$ mmWave channel generated using (2.3) and (2.4) with *on-grid* assumption is shown in Figure 2.3(b). That is, the beamspace channel becomes exactly sparse under the *on-grid* assumption.

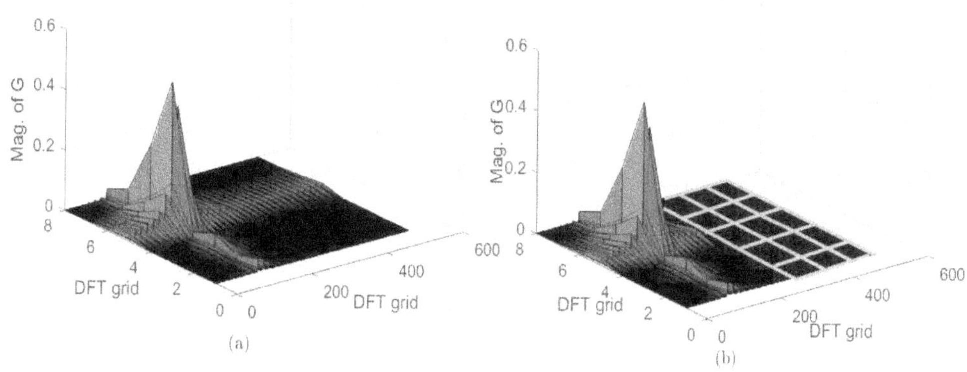

Figure 2.4: (a) Restricted beamspace channel (b) channel sub-matrix of interest

2.5   SEARCH SPACE AWARE CHANNEL MODELING

In this section, we discuss how to incorporate apriori search space restrictions known at the BS and UE while formulating the channel model to accomplish faster cell discovery and channel estimation.   When BS/UE is mounted on a wall or when sector-based antennas are used, there will be restrictions on the directional transmissions/receptions. This information can be used in designing the training phase beamforming weights, thereby scaling down the training overhead and achieving faster cell discovery.

From the channel model discussed in Section 2.4, for every channel multipath with azimuth-elevation AoD pair given by (θ_k^t, ϕ_k^t), the antenna response vectors comprise of the spatial frequencies $\omega cos(\phi_k^t)$ and $\omega sin(\theta_k^t)cos(\phi_k^t)$. Now, if θ_k^t is restricted to be in $[\theta_{min}, \theta_{max}] \forall (k, l)$, then the corresponding spatial frequencies can be represented by a subset of DFT columns from $\mathbf{F}_{N_{t_2}}$. For example, Figure 2.4 shows the beamspace representation of a practical mmWave channel generated using NYUSIM simulator with azimuth angle restricted to $[0 - \pi]$. As shown in Figure 2.4(b), the channel matrix marked in the blue square corresponds to the DFT columns of no interest. The channel

29

gain in this part is insignificant; hence, this part of the beamspace matrix need not be sensed for CD. Let us denote the subset of DFT columns of interest by $\mathbf{Q}_{N_{t_2}}$, which has dimension $N_{t_2} \times Q_{t_2}$. Likewise, the subset of $\mathbf{F}_{N_{t_1}}$ matrix denoted by $\mathbf{Q}_{N_{t_1}}$ of dimension $N_{t_1} \times Q_{t_1}$, can be constructed when $\phi_k \in [\phi_{min}, \phi_{max}]$. Similarly, based on azimuth and elevation restrictions on the receiver size can lead to subsets given by $\mathbf{Q}_{N_{r_1}}$ and $\mathbf{Q}_{N_{r_2}}$. Now, the beamspace matrix corresponding to the restricted AoA-AoD values is given by

$$\mathbf{G}_i^{(r)} = \bar{\mathbf{Q}}_{N_r}^* \mathbf{H}_i \bar{\mathbf{Q}}_{N_t}, \tag{2.5}$$

where $\bar{\mathbf{Q}}_{N_r} = \mathbf{Q}_{N_{r_1}} \otimes \mathbf{Q}_{N_{r_2}}$ and $\bar{\mathbf{Q}}_{N_t} = \mathbf{Q}_{N_{t_1}} \otimes \mathbf{Q}_{N_{t_2}}$. Note that $\mathbf{G}_i^{(r)}$ is a sparse matrix of dimension $Q_{r_1} Q_{r_2} \times Q_{t_1} Q_{t_2}$.

Alike, the restriction of angles of the channel paths at the UE can also be brought into the model. $\mathbf{G}_i^{(r)}$ is of smaller size compared with the unrestricted channel $\mathbf{G}_i$, and hence cell discovery and channel estimation can be made with a lesser number of transmissions.

2.6 SUMMARY

In this chapter, we explained the mmWave system model that will be used to design the beamforming vectors in the subsequent chapters. We then specified the antenna structures and the variations in the input-output model for both ULA and UPA arrays to support 2D and 3D beamforming. We also discussed how to extend the system model for hybrid beamforming architecture to reduce the number of transmissions.

Next, we characterized the mmWave channels using the Saleh-Valenzuala model and studied the sparse nature of mmWave channels in the angle domain. We also explained how to incorporate apriory search space restrictions to the channel model to reduce the training overhead. In the following chapters, we design the beamforming vectors and the receiver algorithm for cell discovery based on the mathematical input-output formulation and the sparse channel model detailed in this chapter.

CHAPTER 3

Cell Discovery and Beam sweeping Techniques

Cell discovery (CD) is the procedure by which user equipment (UE) entering a network finds a suitable (nearby) base station (BS) and its identity in order to establish a link-layer connection. Because of the large path loss, poor propagation characteristics, and the compromised range, unlike in the sub-6GHz systems, the initial cell discovery cannot be done using omnidirectional transmission of synchronization signals in the mmWave systems. Hence, mmWave systems rely on directional signaling for CD, making the cell discovery process very challenging as the large angular space is scanned sequentially. Beam sweeping is a conventional exhaustive CD technique (Barati *et al.*, 2016; Hur *et al.*, 2013), where both transmitter and receiver sweep their beams along the entire angular range (say, 360 degrees) and make a detection based on the angle of arrival (AoA) - angle of departure (AoD) beam-pair corresponding to the largest received signal strength.

In this Chapter, based on the mmWave system and channel model in Chapter 2, first, we present the mathematical model for the cell discovery problem. Then, we elaborately discuss the physical layer implementation of the Conventional Beam Sweep (CBS) scheme by completely specifying its training phase. We also discuss how the beamforming vectors can be modified to implement beam widening or beam combining variations (Beam Combining (BC) method). We analytically characterize the performance of the energy detector at the UE for both beam sweeping and beam combining methods under some channel assumptions. We finally present simulation studies with channels generated using generic mmWave channel emulators and draw inferences on the role of various parameters on CD performance.

3.1 BEAMFORMING TRAINING

Recall the system model in (2.2) in which the UE uses a set of P beamforming vectors, $\{\mathbf{w}_r^{(1)}, \cdots, \mathbf{w}_r^{(P)}\}$, of length N_r and the ith BS uses a set of Q beamforming vectors, $\{\mathbf{w}_{t_i}^{(1)}, \cdots, \mathbf{w}_{t_i}^{(Q)}\}$, of length N_t respectively. For convenience and consistency, we assume the beamforming vectors at BS and UE to be of unit norm. For each beam pair combination (p, q), the ith BS transmits a synchronization signal $\mathbf{x}^{(i)}$ of length N_S, which is specific to its identity i. We assume that the symbols in $\mathbf{x}^{(i)}$ are of unit magnitude. The synchronization signals $\{\mathbf{x}^{(i)}, i \in \{1, \cdots, N_B\}\}$ are chosen such that their cross-correlation is very small. For subsequent use, let us define the maximum cross-correlation as

$$\zeta = \max_{i \neq j} \left| \mathbf{x}^{(i)*} \mathbf{x}^{(j)} \right|. \tag{3.1}$$

With $x_m^{(i)}$ denoting the mth entry of the synchronization signal $\mathbf{x}^{(i)}$, the training phase observations $\{y_{p,q,m}\}$ for $p \in \{1, \cdots, P\}$, $q \in \{1, \cdots, Q\}$ and $m \in \{1, \cdots, N_S\}$ are given by

$$y_{p,q,m} = \mathbf{w}_r^{(p)*} \sum_{i \in \mathcal{A}} \sqrt{\rho_i} \mathbf{H}_i \mathbf{w}_{t_i}^{(q)} x_m^{(i)} + \underbrace{\mathbf{w}_r^{(p)*} \mathbf{n}_{p,q,m}}_{n_{p,q,m}}, \tag{3.2}$$

where ρ_i characterizes the transmit power of ith BS, and $\mathbf{n}_{p,q,m}$ is the additive noise vector. $\mathcal{A}$ denotes the set of unblocked BSs present in the wireless netwrok. Here we omit the index denoting the RF chain for simplicity. We assume, $\mathbf{n}_{p,q,m} \sim$

$\mathcal{CN}(\mathbf{0}, \sigma_n^2 \mathbf{I}_{N_r})$ and hence $n_{p,q,m} \sim \mathcal{CN}(0, \sigma_n^2)$. Note that the total duration of the beamforming training phase is PQN_S. We define the average received SNR of the training phase as

$$\text{SNR} = \frac{\mathbb{E}\left(\sum_{p,q,m} \left| \mathbf{w}_r^{(p)*} \sum_{i \in \mathcal{A}} \sqrt{\rho_i} \mathbf{H}_i \mathbf{w}_{t_i}^{(q)} x_m^{(i)} \right|^2 \right)}{PQN_S \sigma_n^2}, \tag{3.3}$$

where the expectation is taken over many channel realizations.

3.2   CELL DISCOVERY PROBLEM

In the hypothesis testing framework for the cell discovery problem, if the UE receives a signal from the BS, then the channel matrix $\mathbf{H}_i$ in (3.2) is in accordance with the channel model given in (2.3). On the other hand, if the UE does not receive the signal from the BS (when the BS is far away or got blocked by obstacles), the channel matrix, $\mathbf{H} = \mathbf{0}$. Cell discovery problem involves finding the presence (or absence) of BS before initiating the communication link. If the presence of BS is detected, mmWave CD involves finding the AoA-AoD pairs of strong paths with respect to the identified BS. Specifically, using the PQN_s training phase observations in (3.2), UE tries to identify the presence (or absence) of the BS and also find the significant entries in the (Fourier domain) channel matrix $\mathbf{G}_i$, which will give the required AoA-AoD pairs of strong paths of the identified BS.

To solve the CD problem, we need to specify the training phase beamforming weights $\{\mathbf{w}_r^{(p)}, \mathbf{w}_{t_i}^{(q)}\}$ and a detector using the observations $\{y_{p,q,m}\}$. Different choices for beamforming vectors in the training phase lead to different CD techniques.

To address the design of beamforming weights involved during the training phase, we rewrite the observations conveniently as follows. Consider the received signal model by constructing a $P \times Q$ measurement matrix $\mathbf{Y}_m$ in which the observations $y_{p,q,m}$ in (3.2) are stacked as $[\mathbf{Y}_m]_{p,q} = y_{p,q,m}$. Constructing the beamforming matrices, $\mathbf{W}_{t_i} = [\mathbf{w}_{t_i}^{(1)} \ \mathbf{w}_{t_i}^{(2)} \ ... \mathbf{w}_{t_i}^{(Q)}]$ for each i and $\mathbf{W}_r = [\mathbf{w}_r^{(1)} \ \mathbf{w}_r^{(2)} \ ... \mathbf{w}_r^{(P)}]$, we have

$$\mathbf{Y}_m = \sum_{i \in \mathcal{A}} \sqrt{\rho_i} \mathbf{W}_r^* \mathbf{H}_i \mathbf{W}_{t_i} x_m^{(i)} + \mathbf{N}_m; \ m = 1, ..., N_S \tag{3.4}$$

where $\mathbf{N}_m$ is the associated noise matrix. We define *Fourier* domain beamforming matrices $\bar{\mathbf{W}}_{t_i} = \bar{\mathbf{F}}_{N_t}^* \mathbf{W}_{t_i}$ and $\bar{\mathbf{W}}_r = \bar{\mathbf{F}}_{N_r}^* \mathbf{W}_r$ with $\bar{\mathbf{F}}_{N_r} = \mathbf{F}_{N_{r_1}} \otimes \mathbf{F}_{N_{r_2}}$ and $\bar{\mathbf{F}}_{N_t} = \mathbf{F}_{N_{t_1}} \otimes \mathbf{F}_{N_{t_2}}$. Since $\bar{\mathbf{F}}_{N_t}$ and $\bar{\mathbf{F}}_{N_r}$ are unitary matrices obtained from Kronecker product of DFT matrices, the problem of designing the training phase beamforming weights boils down to designing $\bar{\mathbf{W}}_r$ and $\bar{\mathbf{W}}_{t_i}$. Now, using the beamspace channel model explained in (2.4), we rewrite (3.4) as

$$\mathbf{Y}_m = \sum_{i \in \mathcal{A}} \sqrt{\rho_i} \bar{\mathbf{W}}_r^* \mathbf{G}_i \bar{\mathbf{W}}_{t_i} x_m^{(i)} + \mathbf{N}_m; \ m = 1, ..., N_S. \tag{3.5}$$

The above representation is convenient since the beamspace matrices ($\mathbf{G}_i$) are sparse, and the cell discovery problem involves finding the locations of non-zero entries of $\mathbf{G}_i$ for any $i \in \mathcal{A}$. In the next section, we present the conventional beam sweeping (CBS) technique (Barati *et al.*, 2016; Hur *et al.*, 2013) which is being adopted in many wireless standards (Giordani *et al.*, 2019*a*) for the cell discovery problem.

3.3   BEAM SWEEPING SCHEMES

In this method, the transmitter and receiver exhaustively search the optimal AoA-AoD pair by sweeping their beams in the entire $[0, 2\pi]$ space and using all the transmit/receive beam combinations. Different variations of CBS method (Song *et al.*, 2019; Barati *et al.*, 2015; Giordani *et al.*, 2016; Habib *et al.*, 2017) are present in the literature and are being adopted in many wireless standards (Giordani *et al.*, 2019*a*). Channel estimation by sweeping over quantized spatial angles by selecting columns of DFT as training beamforming vectors have been discussed in (Ye *et al.*, 2019; Chung and Kim, 2022). Beam tracking for both slow and fast varying channels using DFT training beams and a MAP-based receiver algorithm is addressed in (Zhang *et al.*, 2019). We use DFT-based beams and employ an energy detector to detect the presence of BS and find the corresponding AoA-AoD pairs.

We also present the beam combining (BC) or beam widening technique (Raghavan *et al.*, 2016), where we widen (by combining multiple beams) the beams used during the training phase so that the overall duration to sweep the entire angular space is reduced. A variation of the BC method by randomly selecting and combining the columns of DFT vectors for beam alignment is proposed in (Khordad *et al.*, 2019). Unlike our proposed method, their scheme does not give an approximate angular path estimate; hence, the post-beamforming SNR will be poor. For both CBS and BC schemes, we analytically characterize the detection and false alarm probabilities with the energy detector under on-grid channel conditions. We also derive the expressions for the probability of cell discovery failure and the average number of cell discovery attempts required by the UE for specialized channel conditions. To the best of our knowledge, such analysis for CBS and BC schemes does not exist in the literature.

3.3.1 Conventional Beam Sweep:

In this scheme, the beamforming vectors along the azimuth and the elevation directions are selected as columns of the unitary DFT matrices of appropriate dimensions. The final beamforming weights are columns of unitary matrices obtained from the Kronecker product of DFT matrices. That is,

$$\mathbf{W}_r = \bar{\mathbf{F}}_{N_r} \text{ and } \mathbf{W}_{t_i} = \bar{\mathbf{F}}_{N_t} \tag{3.6}$$

Note that when a beamforming vector is set as a column of a DFT matrix, the signal radiated by the antenna array is directed at an angle corresponding to the (spatial) frequency given by that column. Here, all the columns of DFT matrices are exhaustively used to span the entire space, and hence $P = N_r$ and $Q = N_t$. Correspondingly, for ULA, the beamforming matrices are $\mathbf{W}_r = \mathbf{F}_{N_r}$ and $\mathbf{W}_t = \mathbf{F}_{N_t}$. This yields the Fourier domain training phase beamforming vectors for both UPA and ULA setup as given below.

$$\bar{\mathbf{W}}_r = \mathbf{I}_{N_r} \text{ and } \bar{\mathbf{W}}_{t_i} = \mathbf{I}_{N_t}, \forall i \tag{3.7}$$

In general, there can be many BSs in the network. Since all the BSs use the same DFT based beamforming matrix, the UE can distinguish between BSs only through the corresponding unique transmit sequence of BSs. In the special condition when a single BS is present in the network, CD can be accomplished without sequence transmission.

For simpler analysis, we assume this simplified set-up with a single BS in the network and CD involves detecting the presence of this BS. Hence, by setting $x_m = x$ the system model can be written as,

$$\mathbf{Y} = \sqrt{\rho}\bar{\mathbf{W}}_r^* \mathbf{G}\bar{\mathbf{W}}_t x + \mathbf{N} = \sqrt{\rho}\mathbf{G}x + \mathbf{N}. \tag{3.8}$$

In terms of the beamforming vector pairs, we get the above model as,

$$y_{p,q} = \sqrt{\rho}[\mathbf{G}]_{p,q}x + n_{p,q,m} \tag{3.9}$$

As noted earlier, the Fourier domain channel matrix $\mathbf{G}$ is approximately sparse. We define the support set $\mathcal{S}$ of $\mathbf{G}$ as,

$$\mathcal{S} = \left\{ (a,b) \middle| |[\mathbf{G}]_{a,b}|^2 > \delta,\, a = 1, ..., N_r; b = 1, ..., N_t \right\}, \tag{3.10}$$

where δ is an appropriately chosen limit value that declares whether or not an entry in matrix G has a considerably large magnitude. For $(p,q) \in \mathcal{S}$, the received symbols $y_{p,q}$ in (3.9), have significant signal component due to sufficiently large channel gains and we term them as *active symbols*. For $(p,q) \notin \mathcal{S}$, the channel gains are close to zero and the corresponding observations are noise dominated.

Now, detecting the presence of at least one accessible BS is equivalent to verifying whether there exists at least one active symbol among $\left\{ y_{p,q}, p \in \{1, ..., N_r\},\ q \in \{1, ..., N_t\} \right\}$. In other words, the BS is detected with transmit-receive beamforming vector pair (p, q) if

$$|y_{p,q}|^2 > \tau, \tag{3.11}$$

where τ is an appropriately chosen threshold. If threshold condition (3.11) is not satisfied for any (p, q) pair, the detector declares that BS is absent. For the above detection rule (3.11), the probability of false alarm $\mathbb{P}_F$ and the probability of successful detection $\mathbb{P}_D$ are given by

$$\mathbb{P}_F \;=\; \mathbb{P}\Big(\bigcup_{(p,q)\notin\mathcal{S}} |y_{p,q}|^2 > \tau\Big), \tag{3.12}$$

$$\mathbb{P}_D \;=\; \mathbb{P}\Big(\bigcup_{(p,q)\in\mathcal{S}} |y_{p,q}|^2 > \tau\Big). \tag{3.13}$$

The threshold τ should be chosen such that $\mathbb{P}_F$ is low.

Theorem 1. *For the conventional beam sweep technique with the energy detector (3.11), under the on-grid channel conditions given in Section 2.4.1, the probability of false alarm is given by*

$$\mathbb{P}_F = 1 - \left(1 - e^{\frac{-\tau}{\sigma_n^2}}\right)^{N_t N_r - |\mathcal{S}|}. \tag{3.14}$$

For the same detector, the probability of successful detection $\mathbb{P}_D$ is given by

$$\mathbb{P}_D = 1 - \prod_{k=1}^{K} \left[1 - \exp\left(-\frac{\tau}{\sigma_n^2 + \rho\sigma_k^2}\right)\right]. \tag{3.15}$$

Proof. Recall that, under *idealized channel assumption*, 2D Fourier domain channel matrix $\mathbf{G}$ will have exactly K non-zero bins. Variance of the non-zero entry in a given DFT bin will be equal to the variance σ_k^2 of the path whose spatial frequency pair matches with the given bin frequency pair. The observations $\{y_{p,q}\}$ from equation (3.9) are given by,

$$
y_{p,q} = \begin{cases} \sqrt{\rho}x[\mathbf{G}]_{p,q} + n_{p,q}, & \text{if } (p,q) \in \mathcal{S}, \\[2em] n_{p,q}, & \text{if } (p,q) \notin \mathcal{S} \end{cases}.
$$

Note that noise samples $\{n_{p,q}\}$ are i.i.d. Gaussian with variance σ_n^2 and $\mathbb{P}(|n_{p,q}|^2 \leq \tau) = \left(1 - e^{-\frac{\tau}{\sigma_n^2}}\right)$. We have,

$$
\begin{aligned}
\mathbb{P}_F &= \mathbb{P}\left(\bigcup_{(p,q)\notin\mathcal{S}} |y_{p,q}|^2 > \tau \right) = 1 - \mathbb{P}\left(\bigcap_{(p,q)\notin\mathcal{S}} |n_{p,q}|^2 \leq \tau \right) \\
&= 1 - \left(1 - e^{-\frac{\tau}{\sigma_n^2}}\right)^{N_t N_r - |\mathcal{S}|}.
\end{aligned}
$$

For any $(p,q) \in \mathcal{S}$, we have $y_{p,q} \sim \mathcal{CN}(0, \rho\sigma_k^2 + \sigma_n^2)$ for some k. In addition, these observations are independent. As the result, the detection probability $\mathbb{P}_D$ is given by,

$$
\begin{aligned}
\mathbb{P}_D &= \mathbb{P}\left(\bigcup_{(p,q)\in\mathcal{S}} |y_{p,q}|^2 > \tau \right) = 1 - \mathbb{P}\left(\bigcap_{(p,q)\in\mathcal{S}} |y_{p,q}|^2 \leq \tau \right) \\
&= 1 - \prod_{(p,q)\in\mathcal{S}} \mathbb{P}(|y_{p,q}|^2 \leq \tau) \\
&= 1 - \prod_{k\in\{1,\cdots,K\}} \left(1 - e^{-\frac{\tau}{\rho\sigma_k^2+\sigma_n^2}}\right).
\end{aligned}
$$

$\square$

We note that, asymptotically as $\sigma_n^2 \longrightarrow 0$, $\mathbb{P}_D \longrightarrow 1$ and $\mathbb{P}_F \longrightarrow 0$. We point out that the assumption of *on-grid conditions* is needed only for deriving the analytical expressions for $\mathbb{P}_D$. However, the training schemes and the detectors are also applicable for practical (off-grid) mmWave channels, which is substantiated by the simulation studies in Section 3.5.

Selection of Threshold

In (3.11), the test statistic in the left hand side of the equation is the received signal energy corresponding to a particular transmit-receive beam pair. The threshold τ in the detector (3.11) is set as $\kappa\sigma_n^2$, where κ is chosen such that the probability of false alarm $\mathbb{P}_F$ (which is the probability of identifying an inactive BS and/or identifying incorrect AoD-AoA pair) is at most 0.01. Hence, our criteria for detection is equivalent to the detection rules followed in (Soleimani *et al.*, 2018; Giordani *et al.*, 2019*b*,*a*) where received SNR is compared with the fixed threshold. Note that the value of κ, in general, will be different for various beamforming techniques and parameters like number of measurements, beam resolution etc.

In simulations, first we take the mean of the total signal energy across all the bins over all the channel iterations and calculate σ_n^2 to meet a particular SNR. Then, we vary κ in simulations to fix $\mathbb{P}_F$ as 0.01.

3.3.2 Beam Combining method:

CBS incurs a large training overhead ($N_t N_r N_S$) as it does not exploit the sparseness of the beamspace channel matrix. We present the details of beam combining (BC) or beam widening technique (Raghavan *et al.*, 2016), where we widen (by combining multiple beams) the beams used during the training phase. This helps to reduce the overall duration to sweep the entire angular space. A direct approach to widen the beams for scanning the space is to employ training beamforming vectors that are constructed as (weighted) linear combination of the columns of $\mathbf{F}_{N_t}$ and $\mathbf{F}_{N_r}$ matrices at the BS and UE respectively. Specifically, for an integer α which divides N_t, we define an $N_t \times \frac{N_t}{\alpha}$ *combining* matrix, $\mathbf{S}_{N_t,\alpha} = \frac{1}{\sqrt{\alpha}}[\mathbf{I}_{\frac{N_t}{\alpha}} \otimes \mathbf{1}_\alpha]$. Note that the scaling factor $\frac{1}{\sqrt{\alpha}}$ ensures that columns are of unit norm. Similarly, we define $N_r \times \frac{N_r}{\beta}$ matrix $\mathbf{S}_{N_r,\beta} = \frac{1}{\sqrt{\beta}}[\mathbf{I}_{\frac{N_t}{\beta}} \otimes \mathbf{1}_\beta]$. With $P = \frac{N_r}{\beta}$, $Q = \frac{N_t}{\alpha}$, we define the beamforming weights as,

$$\bar{\mathbf{W}}_r = \mathbf{S}_{N_r,\beta}$$

$$\bar{\mathbf{W}}_{t_i} = \mathbf{S}_{N_t,\alpha}, \forall i. \tag{3.16}$$

Compared to the CBS method, BC has reduced the training overhead by a factor of $\alpha\beta$. The magnitude of the entries of the beamforming vectors will no longer be the same. Hence, the designed BC scheme cannot be realized with phase shifters alone. However, BC scheme can be easily implemented through digital and hybrid precoding architectures (O. E. Ayach, S. Rajagopal, S. Abu-Surra, Z. Pi and R. W. Heath, 2014; Lee *et al.*, 2016*b*).

With the above beamforming vectors, the observation model in (3.8) for a single BS scenario without SS transmission becomes

$$\mathbf{Y} = \sqrt{\rho}\mathbf{G}^{(w)}x + \mathbf{N}, \tag{3.17}$$

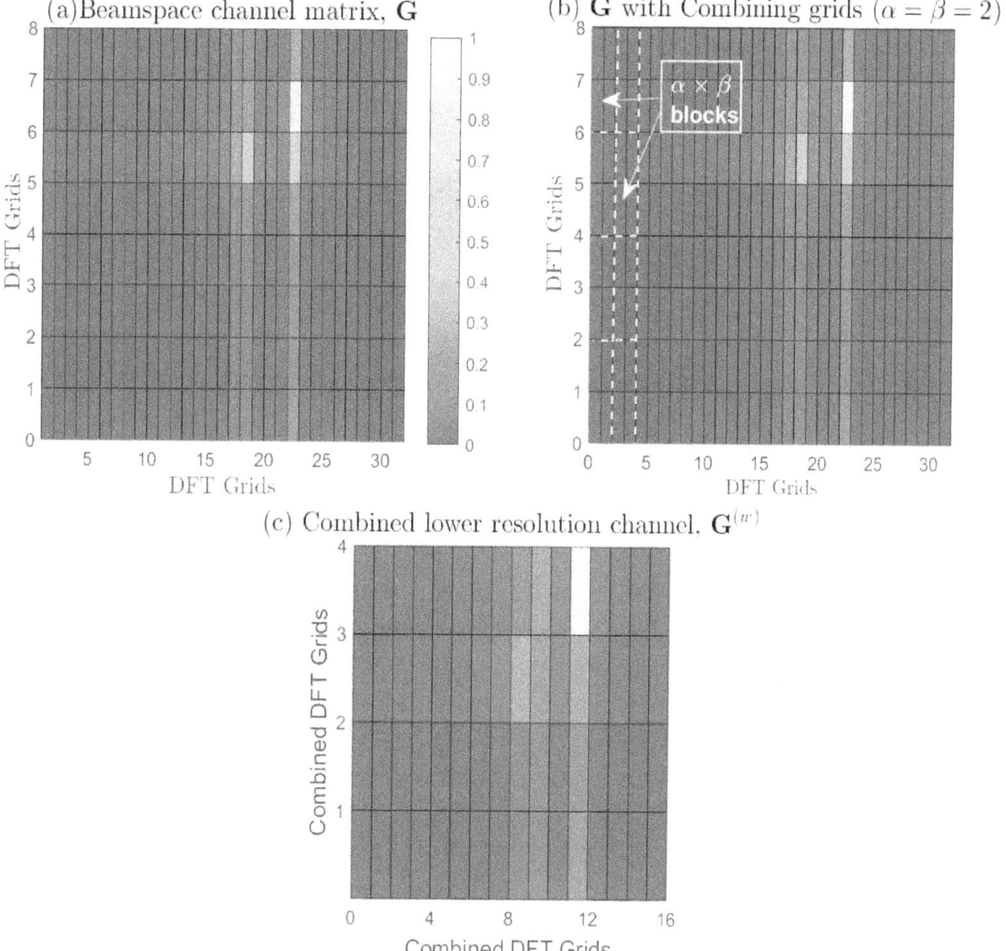

where the *low resolution* beamspace matrix based on wider beams

$$\mathbf{G}^{(w)} = \mathbf{S}^*_{N_r,\beta} \mathbf{G} \mathbf{S}_{N_t,\alpha}, \tag{3.18}$$

is obtained by grouping and adding entries from the finer beamspace matrix $\mathbf{G}_i$. Note that,

$$[\mathbf{G}^{(w)}]_{a,b} = \sum_{k=(a-1)\beta+1}^{a\beta} \sum_{l=(b-1)\alpha+1}^{b\alpha} \frac{1}{\sqrt{\alpha\beta}} [\mathbf{G}]_{k,l}. \tag{3.19}$$

Essentially, this design considers the channel entries within α bins along the transmit direction and β bins along the receiver direction as shown in Figure 3.1(b). Then, these entries are then grouped into a single combined measurement as shown in Figure 3.1.

Compared to the CBS scheme, which searches for non-zero entries in the finer grid, the BC scheme has lesser training overhead scaled by a factor of $\alpha\beta$. In this design, it is also possible to group α_1 bins along azimuth and α_2 bins along elevation separately for UPA by setting $\bar{\mathbf{W}}_{t_i}$ as

$$\mathbf{S}_{N_{t_1},N_{t_2},\alpha_1,\alpha_2} = \frac{1}{\sqrt{\alpha_1}} \left[\mathbf{I}_{\frac{N_{t_1}}{\alpha_1}} \otimes \mathbf{1}_{\alpha_1}\right] \otimes \frac{1}{\sqrt{\alpha_2}} \left[\mathbf{I}_{\frac{N_{t_2}}{\alpha_2}} \otimes \mathbf{1}_{\alpha_2}\right]. \tag{3.20}$$

When we are using wider beams, the directivity of the transmission decreases, and the overall beamforming gain reduces. In order to see that, consider $g_{\max} = \max_{p,q} \mathbb{E}\left|[\mathbf{G}]_{p,q}\right|^2$, which is the maximum variance for the entries of the beamspace matrix $\mathbf{G}$, assuming that they are all zero-mean. The beamspace matrix typically exhibits a block sparse structure (Manoj and Kannu, 2018) due to the spectral leakage into the nearby DFT bins corresponding to the actual AoA-AoD pairs of the channel paths. Since the leakage has sinc structure, the leakage terms around the true AoA-AoD pair can have the same or different signs. With the assumption that the entries in the summation in (3.19) are uncorrelated, the maximum variance for the entries in the low-resolution beamspace matrix $\mathbf{G}^{(w)}$ will be smaller than $g_{\max}$ as $\sum_{k=(a-1)\beta+1}^{a\beta} \sum_{l=(b-1)\alpha+1}^{b\alpha} \frac{1}{\alpha\beta}\mathbb{E}\left|[\mathbf{G}]_{k,l}\right|^2 \leq g_{\max}$. This leads to a reduction in the beamforming gain. This argument is substantiated further using simulation results in Section 3.5.

Now, the active set $\mathcal{S}_{\mathrm{BC}}$ is defined as the set of indices $\{(a,b)\}$ for which the corresponding low-resolution beamspace matrix $[\mathbf{G}]_{a,b}^{(w)}$ in (3.19) has contribution from at least one non-zero channel entry from the support set $\mathcal{S}$ of the channel matrix $\mathbf{G}$, which is given in (3.10). Then, we have, $\mathcal{S}_{\mathrm{BC}} = \{(a,b)\big|\mathcal{S}_{a,b} \cap \mathcal{S} \neq \emptyset\}$.

We employ the energy detector rule (3.11) to detect the presence of the active BS. If the index (a,b) is detected, the DFT bin indices from the set $\mathcal{S}_{a,b}$ give the associated AoA-AoD pairs. For the BC technique, the resolutions of the detected transmit and receive beams are wider by a factor of α and β, respectively, compared to the CBS scheme. Note that the effective channel for a combined beam is the sum of channel gains of the constituent AoA- AoD pairs. If the effective channel is small due to the destructive addition of the beam space channel coefficients, then it may lead to a miss-detection for BC scheme for higher α and β values.

Theorem 2. *Under ideal on-grid channel conditions in Section 2.4.1, the false alarm* *probability for the BC scheme is*

$$\mathbb{P}_F \;=\; 1 - \left(1 - e^{\frac{-\tau}{\sigma_n^2}}\right)^{\frac{N_t N_r}{\alpha\beta} - |\mathcal{S}_{BC}|}, \tag{3.21}$$

The probability of detecting the BS is lower bounded as

$$\mathbb{P}_D \geq \exp\left(-\frac{\tau}{\sigma_n^2 + \frac{\rho}{\alpha\beta}\max_k \sigma_k^2}\right). \tag{3.22}$$

Proof. Under ideal channel assumptions, out of the $\frac{N_t N_r}{\alpha\beta}$ observations in (3.17), only symbols associated with $\mathcal{S}_{BC}$ have contributions from the non-zero channel gain. Rest of the observations are purely i.i.d. Gaussian noise. The false alarm probability for the BC scheme (when at least one of the noise samples crosses the threshold) is obtained in the same manner as in Theorem 1. Detection happens if any one of $y_{p,q}$ for $(p,q) \in \mathcal{S}_{BC}$ crosses the energy threshold τ in (3.11). Let $\sigma_{p,q}^2$ denote the signal variance of $y_{p,q}$, which is defined as the variance of the $\frac{\sqrt{\rho x}}{\sqrt{\alpha\beta}}[\mathbf{G}^{(w)}]_{p,q}$. We note that $\max_{(p,q)} \sigma_{p,q}^2 \geq \frac{\rho}{\alpha\beta}\max_k \sigma_k^2$. At least one entry $y_{p,q}$ has signal variance $\sigma_{p,q}^2 \geq \frac{\rho}{\alpha\beta}\max_k \sigma_k^2$. Hence the detection probability is lower bounded by the probability of a Gaussian random variable with variance $\frac{\rho}{\alpha\beta}\max_k \sigma_k^2$ crossing the energy threshold τ, as given in (3.22). $\qquad\square$

3.3.3 Analysis on CD failure & Time complexity

Cell search, in general, is not a one-time attempt. BSs transmit pilot signals at regular time instants to provide chances for UEs to get connected to them. We declare CD failure only if the UE is not able to detect at least one active BS within N_{max} attempts. N_{max} depends on how fast the channel varies and is directly related to the coherence time of the channel. The multi-path arrival and departure angles vary slowly when compared with the channel gains. We assume the AoA-AoD of the channels remain the same (thus $\mathcal{S}$), and only the channel gain varies during N_{max} attempts. We use the probability of CD failure, $\mathbb{P}_{fail}$, to quantify the CD failure and characterize it in Theorem 3.

Theorem 3. *Under ideal on-grid channel conditions in Section 2.4.1, the probability of CD failure for the CBS scheme can be written as,*

$$\mathbb{P}_{fail} = (1 - \mathbb{P}_D)^{N_{max}} \tag{3.23}$$

where expression for $\mathbb{P}_D$ is given in (3.15). Similarly, the lower bound on $\mathbb{P}_{fail}$ can be derived for BC scheme using the upper bound on $\mathbb{P}_D$ (obtained in equation (3.22)).

Proof. $\mathbb{P}_{fail}$ is the probability of CD failure in all the N_{max} repeated trials. Since the statistics of the channel paths remain unchanged for every trial, each trial will have a probability of detecting at least an accessible BS equal to $\mathbb{P}_D$. Further, every trial is independent of another. Applying these results, we obtain the expression as in Theorem 3. It is clear from the expression that $\mathbb{P}_{fail}$ decreases with increase in $\mathbb{P}_D$ and N_{max}. As $N_{max} \to \infty$, it means that the trial is repeated a large number of times, and $\mathbb{P}_{fail} \to 0$.

$\square$

A measure of time complexity that is closely related with $\mathbb{P}_{fail}$ is the average number of attempts (N_{avg}) made for the first detection, within the maximum number of attempts fixed as N_{max}. N_{avg} for any scheme will be analogous to its $\mathbb{P}_D$ value and will decrease with increase in $\mathbb{P}_D$. N_{avg} for CBS and BC schemes are characterized in Theorem 4.

Theorem 4. *With $\mathbb{P}_D$ defined as in Theorem 1 for CBS scheme, for a fixed $\mathbb{P}_F$, N_{avg} within a maximum of N_{max} attempts can be derived as,*

$$N_{avg} = \frac{1}{\mathbb{P}_D} - \frac{N_{max}(1 - \mathbb{P}_D)^{N_{max}}}{1 - (1 - \mathbb{P}_D)^{N_{max}}} \tag{3.24}$$

Proof. Let N be the random variable indicating the number of trials required to see the "first detection" and let Q be the event that $N \leq N_{max}$. Then, N follows geometric distribution and the probability mass function (pmf) of $N = n$ is given by $\mathbb{P}(N = n) = (1 - \mathbb{P}_D)^{n-1}\mathbb{P}_D, \forall n$ where $\mathbb{P}_D$ is the CD probability of detecting at least one BS in an attempt. Probability of the event Q is $1 - (1 - \mathbb{P}_D)^{N_{max}}$. Conditional pmf of the number of attempts given the event Q can be then derived as,

$$\begin{aligned}
\mathbb{P}(N = n \mid Q) &= \frac{\mathbb{P}(Q \mid N = n)\mathbb{P}(N = n)}{\mathbb{P}(Q)} \\
&= \frac{1.(1 - \mathbb{P}_D)^{n-1}\mathbb{P}_D}{\mathbb{P}(Q)}, 1 \leq n \leq N_{max}
\end{aligned}$$

Now, avg. number of trials needed will be,

$$\begin{aligned}
N_{avg} = \mathbb{E}[N \mid Q] &= \sum_{k=1}^{N_{max}} k\mathbb{P}(N = k \mid Q) \\
&= \sum_{k=1}^{N_{max}} k\frac{\mathbb{P}_D(1 - \mathbb{P}_D)^{k-1}}{\mathbb{P}(Q)} \\
&= \frac{1}{\mathbb{P}(Q)}\left(\mathbb{P}_D - N_{max}(1 - \mathbb{P}_D)^{N_{max}}\right) \\
&= \frac{1}{\mathbb{P}_D} - \frac{N_{max}(1 - \mathbb{P}_D)^{N_{max}}}{1 - (1 - \mathbb{P}_D)^{N_{max}}}.
\end{aligned}$$

Substituting $\mathbb{P}_D$ expressions in Theorem 1 and Theorem 2, analytical expression and bound for N_{avg} can be obtained for CBS and BC schemes respectively. Note that, as N_{max} becomes large, the second term in the N_{avg} expression vanishes, and $N_{avg} \approx \frac{1}{\mathbb{P}_D}$ which is the expectation of the geometric distribution with parameter $\mathbb{P}_D$. $\qquad\square$

Substituting $\mathbb{P}_D$ expressions in Theorem 1 and Theorem 2, analytical expression and bound for N_{avg} can be obtained for CBS and BC schemes, respectively. Note that, as N_{max} becomes large, the second term in the N_{avg} expression vanishes, and $N_{avg} \approx \frac{1}{\mathbb{P}_D}$ which is the expectation of the geometric distribution with parameter $\mathbb{P}_D$.

3.4 BEAM SWEEP WITH SEQUENCE TRANSMISSION

In many communication systems (a cellular network, for example), there are multiple base stations (BSs) in the network, with each BS given a unique identity. In the cell discovery problem with multiple BS, the UE needs to find the presence of at least one suitable BS from which the UE has sufficient received signal strength to establish a communication link. In addition, the UE also needs to find the identity of the detected BS and the corresponding AoA-AoD pairs. Each BS is assigned a unique sequence in a cellular network, referred to as a Synchronization Sequence (SS), based on its identity. Each BS periodically transmits its unique synchronization sequence in order to facilitate cell discovery. In 5G-NR standards, the mmWave systems are envisioned to transmit synchronization sequence along with directional beamforming (Giordani *et al.*, 2019*a*). In this Section, we consider multiple BS and present details of the beam sweeping along with the transmission of SS. We analyze the detection performance of the energy detector for orthogonal SS under on-grid channel assumptions.

3.4.1 Synchronization Sequences

Consider a network with N_B unique base stations, with their identities from the set $\mathcal{I} = \{1, \cdots, N_B\}$. Let $\mathcal{X} = \{\mathbf{x}_1, \cdots, \mathbf{x}_{N_B}\}$, each $\mathbf{x}_m$ being an $N_S \times 1$ vector, denote the set of synchronization sequences (SS) used by the BSs (BS with identity $m \in \mathcal{I}$ is assigned a SS $\mathbf{x}_m$). Orthogonal sequences are good candidates for synchronization sequences. In this case, $\mathbf{x}_m^* \mathbf{x}_n = 0$ for any $m, n \in \mathcal{I}$ with $m \neq n$. However, the orthogonal SS requires that $N_S \geq N_B$. In a network with a large number of BSs (say, a cellular network), the requirement $N_S \geq N_B$ is undesirable due to the large overhead for transmitting SS. Hence, non-orthogonal signals with small cross-correlation are used as SSs. We discuss some of the SSs used in existing wireless standards.

Zadoff-Chu (ZC) sequences are commonly used as synchronization signals due to their good correlation properties (Mashud and Kaushik, 2017). Let $\mathbf{s}_0, \mathbf{s}_1, ..., \mathbf{s}_{L-1}$ be root ZC sequences (with norm as $\sqrt{L}$) of length L with L being an odd prime number. The kth value of rth root ZC sequence is given as $s_r(k) = e^{-i\pi r \frac{k(k+1)}{L}}, 0 \leq k \leq L - 1$. If $\mathbf{s}_r^{(l)}$ denote the lth cyclic shift of $\mathbf{s}_r$ with $l = 0, 1, ..., L - 1$ and $r = 1, ..., L - 1$, then

1. $\left(\mathbf{s}_r^{(l_1)}\right)^* \left(\mathbf{s}_r^{(l_2)}\right) = 0, \forall l_1 \neq l_2.$

2. $\left(\mathbf{s}_{r_1}^{(l)}\right)^* \left(\mathbf{s}_{r_2}^{(l)}\right) = \sqrt{L}, \forall r_1 \neq r_2 \& r_1, r_2 = 1, ..., L - 1.$

The cyclic shifts of the root sequences can also be considered as ZC sequences. The first sequence $\mathbf{s}_0$ is an all-one sequence $\mathbf{1}_L$, and the shifted versions cannot be used as

SS. Hence, in total, we can have $L(L-1)+1$ ZC sequences of odd prime length L with good correlation properties. Gold codes can also be used for synchronization purposes because of their good cross-correlation properties (Aditi *et al.*, 2020). In this chapter, we use ZC sequences as synchronization signals for multiple BS case.

3.4.2   Beam Sweep with Synchronization Signals

The received signal model for the CBS technique coupled with SS transmission for multiple BSs is given in (3.5) and can be written as given below in terms of beamforming vector pair (p, q).

$$y_{p,q,m} = \sum_{i \in \mathcal{A}} \sqrt{\rho_i}[\mathbf{G}_i]_{p,q} x_m^{(i)} + n_{p,q,m}.$$
(3.25)

Note that the above equation is valid for both UPA and ULA-based mmWave systems. We obtain a total of $N_t N_r N_S$ number of observations for the training phase. Since all the base stations use the same beamforming weights, the receiver needs to differentiate the BSs based on the synchronization signals. Towards CD, we correlate this set of observations with SS from each BS, in each beam direction. For $p \in \{1, \cdots, N_r\}, q \in \{1, \cdots, N_t\}, i \in \{1, \cdots, N_B\}$, the correlation test statistic corresponding to the $(p, q)^{th}$ bin of BS identity i denoted by $z_{p,q,i}$, is computed as follows.

$$z_{p,q,i} = \sum_{m=1}^{N_S} y_{p,q,m} x_m^{(i)*}.$$
(3.26)

The receiver declares an AoA-AoD pair bin $(\bar{p}, \bar{q})$ corresponding to BS identity $\bar{i}$ to be *active* according to the energy detector rule if,

$$|z_{\bar{p},\bar{q},\bar{i}}|^2 > \tau, \qquad (3.27)$$

where τ is a suitably chosen threshold as described in Section 3.3.1. In a similar manner, we can incorporate SS transmission and detection with the BC scheme as well. The received SNR for the training phase of the above reception model is given in (3.3).

3.4.3 Analysis of CBS with orthogonal SS

In order to analytically characterize the $\mathbb{P}_F$ and $\mathbb{P}_D$ of the energy detector in (3.27), we make some additional assumptions. As before, we consider on-grid channels for active BS such that, for $i \in \mathcal{A}$, $\mathbf{G}_i$ has exactly K_i independent Gaussian entries with variances $\sigma_{k,i}^2$. We also assume that SS of different BS are mutually orthogonal, such that $\mathbf{x}_i^* \mathbf{x}_m = 0$, for $i \neq m$. Under these assumptions, we have

$$z_{p,q,m} = \sum_{\ell=1}^{N_S} \left(\sum_{i \in \mathcal{A}} \sqrt{\rho_i} [\mathbf{G}_i]_{p,q} x_{i,\ell} + n_{p,q,\ell} \right) x_{m,\ell}^* \qquad (3.28)$$

$$= \sum_{i \in \mathcal{A}} \sqrt{\rho_i} [\mathbf{G}_i]_{p,q} \sum_{\ell=1}^{N_S} x_{i,\ell} x_{m,\ell}^* + \underbrace{\sum_{\ell=1}^{N_S} n_{p,q,\ell} x_{m,\ell}^*}_{\tilde{n}_{p,q,m}}. \qquad (3.29)$$

Due to the orthogonality and unit modulus assumptions on SS, we have

$$\sum_{\ell=1}^{N_S} x_{i,\ell} x_{m,\ell}^* = \begin{cases} 0 & i \neq m, \\ N_S & i = m, \end{cases} \qquad (3.30)$$

and hence $z_{p,q,m} = \sqrt{\rho_m} N_S [\mathbf{G}_m]_{p,q} + \tilde{n}_{p,q,m}$. Note $\tilde{n}_{p,q,m}$ are i.i.d. Gaussian with variance $N_S \sigma_n^2$. Also, note that $[\mathbf{G_m}]_{p,q}$ is non-zero only if $m \in \mathcal{A}$ and 2D DFT bin pair (p, q) corresponds to one of the non-zero multipaths gains in $\mathbf{G}_m$. Out of the $N_t N_r N_S$ correlation metrics $\{z_{p,q,m}\}$, only $K_{\text{tot}} = \sum_{i \in \mathcal{A}} K_i$ of the metrics have non-zero channel gains. The rest of the metrics are purely i.i.d. Gaussian noise. Based on this observation, we have the following theorem, which can be proved in the same manner as Theorem 1.

Theorem 5. *For the conventional beam sweep technique with orthogonal synchronization transmission, under the on-grid channel conditions, the probability of false alarm is given by*

$$\mathbb{P}_F = 1 - \left(1 - e^{\frac{-\tau}{N_S \sigma_n^2}}\right)^{N_t N_r N_B - K_{tot}}, \tag{3.31}$$

and the probability of successful detection $\mathbb{P}_D$ is given by

$$\mathbb{P}_D = 1 - \prod_{i \in \mathcal{A}} \prod_{k=1}^{K_i} \left[1 - \exp\left(-\frac{\tau}{N_S \sigma_n^2 + \rho_i N_S^2 \sigma_{k,i}^2}\right)\right]. \tag{3.32}$$

3.5 SIMULATION RESULTS

In this section, we present our simulation results evaluating the performance of CBS and BC CD algorithms in terms of probability of successful detection $\mathbb{P}_D$, probability of CD failure $\mathbb{P}_{fail}$, and average number of attempts for CD success N_{avg} with a constraint on the probability of false alarm $\mathbb{P}_F$.

3.5.1   Simulation Setup & Channel Generation:

For simulation, we consider N_B number of BSs to be randomly deployed around the UE within a radial distance of R meters. Out of these BSs, we randomly select a set of N_A active BSs from which the signals reach the given UE. Let N_A denote the size of $\mathcal{A}$, which denotes the number of active BSs in the neighborhood of the given UE. The remaining inactive BSs are assumed to have zero channel gain with the UE.

We generate the mmWave channel matrices using NYUSIM simulator (Version 3.1) (Sun *et al.*, 2017; Rappaport *et al.*, 2017) which is an experimentally driven spatial channel simulator for mmWave communication systems. The simulator has been developed based on extensive real-world channel measurements and can be used for carrier frequencies ranging from 500 MHz to 100 GHz, and RF bandwidths from 0 to 800 MHz. The channels between the active BSs and the UE obtained, in this case, are not *on-grid channels*. Further, the channels can be LoS or NLoS, and are determined based on the NYUSIM LoS probability model discussed in (Rappaport *et al.*, 2017). We set the operating carrier frequency as 28 GHz, set up as "Urban Micro scenario" with $R = 50$ and system bandwidth $= 5$ MHz. The symbol duration is chosen to be $0.4\mu s$, which is much larger than the maximum delay spread given in (Deng *et al.*, 2015) at 28GHz, and hence our narrowband assumption is justified. All other parameters in the NYUSIM Graphical User Interface are set to their default values. Note that, even though the system bandwidth may be large, the training signals for cell discovery can be transmitted over a smaller band. For instance, in LTE standards, the synchronization signals are transmitted over a bandwidth of 1 MHz, while the system bandwidth can be up to 20 MHz. Further, the Frobenius norm of the channel matrix between any BS

Table 3.1: Summary of Simulation settings

Parameters	Values in Simulations
NYUSIM Parameters	
Scenario	Urban Micro
Narrowband Bandwidth	5 MHz
Carrier frequency	28 GHz
Cell radius	50 meters
Multipath elevation AoD range	$-\frac{\pi}{2}$ to $\frac{\pi}{2}$
Multipath azimuth AoD range	0 to π
Antenna Dimensions	
UPA	$N_t = 32 \times 16, N_r = 4 \times 2$
ULA	$N_t = 64, N_r = 8$
Algorithm Design	
Prob. of false alarm	0.01

and UE is normalized to 1. The transmit power levels, ρ_is, used at different BSs also result in variation in their respective received signal strength at the UE. We fix $\rho_i \forall i$ as a random number between 1 to 10. Hence, the maximum difference between the power levels of the strongest and weakest active BS will be 10dB.

We set the non-zero channel entry threshold in (3.10) as $\delta = \frac{1}{2}\left(\max_{a,b} \left| [\mathbf{G}_i]_{a,b} \right|^2 \right)$, that is, any entry within 3 dB of the absolute square of the largest magnitude entry in $\mathbf{G}_i$ is considered a non-zero entry. The threshold τ in the detector (3.11) and (3.27) is set as $\kappa \sigma_n^2$, where κ is chosen such that the probability of false alarm $\mathbb{P}_F$ is at most 0.01. Note that the value of κ, in general, will be different for different techniques.

For UPA scenarios, we set $N_t = 32 \times 16$ and $N_r = 4 \times 2$, and for ULA case $N_t = 64$ and $N_r = 8$ respectively. To be aligned with the practical setup, the multipath azimuth and elevation AoDs are restricted to $[0 - \pi]$ and $[-\frac{\pi}{2}, \frac{\pi}{2}]$ respectively while generating mmWave channels using NYUSIM simulator. Also, as mentioned in Section 2.3, the number of transmissions required to exhaust all the pairs of P receive and Q transmit

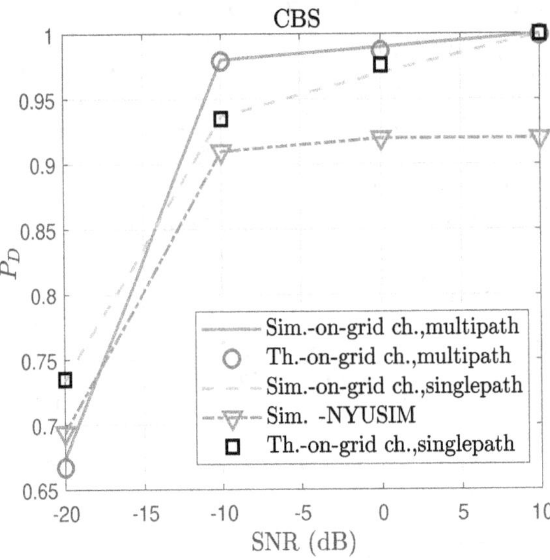

Figure 3.2: Comparison of the analytical and simulated $\mathbb{P}_D$ along with NYUSIM results for CBS.

beamforming weights will be $M = \frac{PQ}{N_{\text{rf}}}$. Unless mentioned, we fix $N_{\text{rf}} = 4$ and UPA set-up with restricted channel conditions for simulations. We assume all widening of the beams to be done at the transmitter by setting the reduction parameter $\beta = 1$. M is the training overhead which indicates the time required for CD and is given by $M = \frac{N_t N_r}{\alpha_1 \alpha_2 N_{\text{rf}}}$. The simulation settings are summarised in 4.1 for reference.

3.5.2 Verifying the derived expressions using simulations:

We verify the $\mathbb{P}_D$ expressions derived for the CBS and BC schemes using simulations in Figure 3.2 and Figure 3.3. We plot the $\mathbb{P}_D$ curves for *on-grid channel* set-up (in all the Figures), as a function of SNR which is defined as, $\text{SNR} = \frac{\sum_{i=1}^{N_A} \sum_{k_i=1}^{K_i} \rho_i \sigma_{k_i}^2}{N_t N_r \sigma_n^2}$ with channel gains distributed as $\mathcal{CN}(0, \sigma_{k_i}^2)$. Here, $\sigma_{k_i}^2 = \frac{N_t N_r}{K_i} \alpha_{k,i}$ and $\alpha_{k_i} \in (0, 1)$, $\forall k_i$. We fix $N_A = N_B = 1$. We consider multi-path scenario with $K = 3$ and for single-path scenario, K is set to 1. From Figure 3.2, we observe that for *ideal channel*

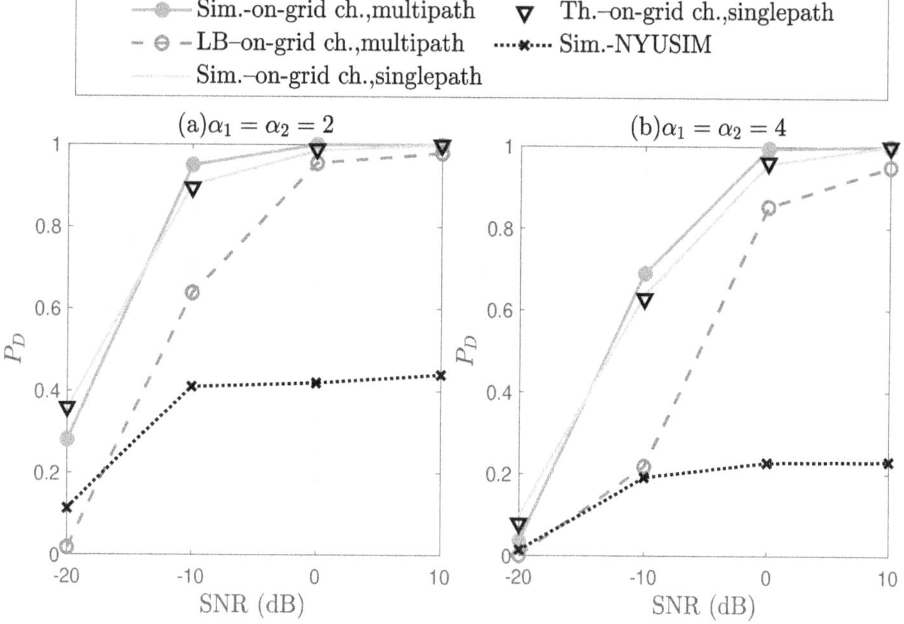

Figure 3.3: Comparison of the analytical and simulated $\mathbb{P}_D$ along with NYUSIM results for BC.

conditions both analytical and simulation results exactly match for the CBS scheme. In addition, we also plot the $\mathbb{P}_D$ performance obtained using the NYUSIM channels (which are not on-grid) with the SNR defined in (3.3), and observe the close similarity with the performance of multipath *ideal channel* set-up. We analyze the analytical and simulation results for the BC scheme with different α_1 and α_2 values in Figure 3.3(a) and Figure 3.3(b) for different beam widths. BC scheme uses widened/combined beams for exhaustive search and hence has reduced training overhead ($\alpha_1 = \alpha_2 = 2 \implies M = 256$; $\alpha_1 = \alpha_2 = 4 \implies M = 64$) compared to the CBS scheme (which requires $M = 1024$). From (3.22), the lower bound for $\mathbb{P}_D$ is met with equality when the channel contains a single path (i.e., $K = 1$). This is also verified through simulation in Figure 3.3.

We plot the $\mathbb{P}_D$ performance of CBS with orthogonal sequence based transmissions in Figure 3.4 with respect to SNR. We set $N_A = 4$ and $K_i - \{3, 4, 2, 2\}$ for $i \in A$. Here

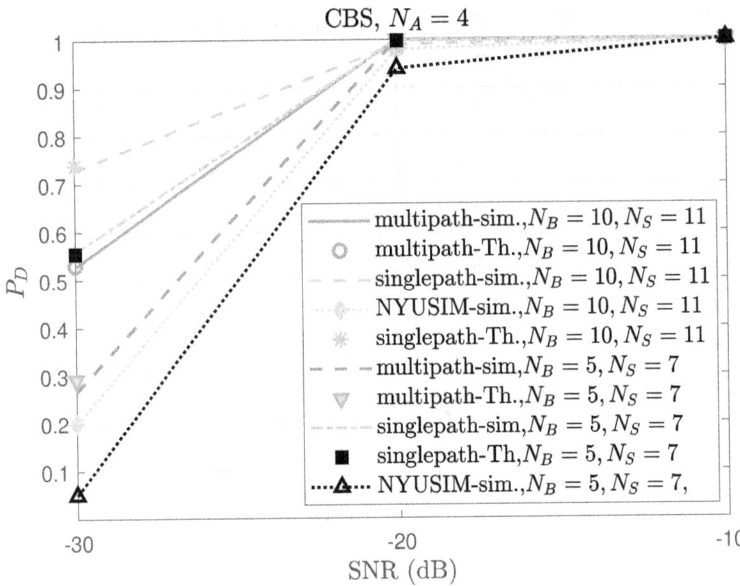

Figure 3.4: Comparison of the analytical $\mathbb{P}_D$ expressions with NYUSIM results for BS with sequence transmission.

too, we see that the analytical (3.32) and simulation results match for the *ideal channel condition*. We verify the same for $N_B = 10, N_S = 11$ case and $N_B = 5, N_S = 7$ case. Also, the analytical $\mathbb{P}_D$ plot closely matches the performance obtained using mmWave channels generated with NYUSIM for higher SNRs.

3.5.3 Performance of CBS and BC schemes for practical channels

We plot $\mathbb{P}_D$ vs SNR for mmWave channels generated using NYUSIM in Figure 3.5(a) and Figure 3.6(a) for UPA and ULA antenna configurations respectively. We fix $N_B = 100, N_A = 4$ and $N_S = 11$. Being an exhaustive search mechanism, the CBS scheme outperforms BC but at the expense of large training overhead. BC scheme uses widened/combined beams for exhaustive search and hence has reduced training overhead. As we increase the overall reduction factor $\alpha_1 \alpha_2$, the resolution of the

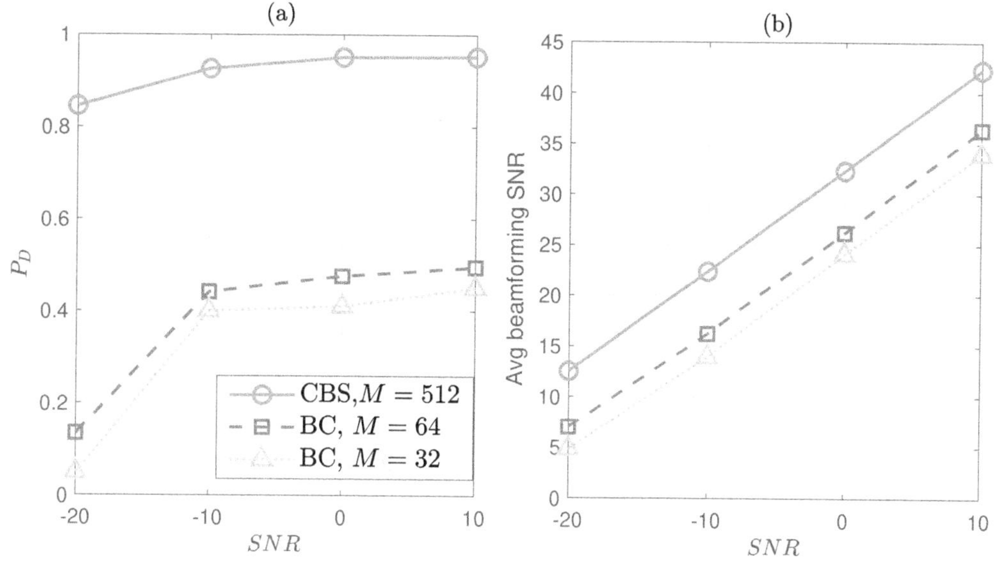

Figure 3.5: (a) Detect at least 1 active BS using sequence transmission. (b)Average beamforming SNR for the detected BS. Parameters are fixed as $N_A = 4$, $N_B = 100$ and $N_S = 11$ with UPA set up.

estimated AoA-AoD decreases, affecting the detection performance for the BC method.

After CD, let the detected BS identity be i_0 and the corresponding AoA-AoD pair be (p_0, q_0). Now, we plot the *average beamforming SNR* achieved using the beamforming vectors directed to the detected BS i_0 with the detected AoA-AoD pair (p_0, q_0) for various training schemes. Specifically, with $\mathbf{w}_t = [\bar{\mathbf{F}}_{N_t}]_{:,q_0}$ and $\mathbf{w}_r = [\bar{\mathbf{F}}_{N_r}]_{:,p_0}$ being the beamforming directions, we define the beamforming SNR as, $\dfrac{\left| \sqrt{\rho_{i_0}} \, \mathbf{w}_r^H \mathbf{H}_{i_0} \mathbf{w}_t \right|^2}{\sigma_n^2}$. We average this beamforming SNR over all the detected BSs for multiple channel realizations under the condition that the detected BS is an active one.

Figure 3.5(b) and Figure 3.6(b) shows the variation of average beamforming SNR with respect to received SNR for different CD schemes, given successful detection. For

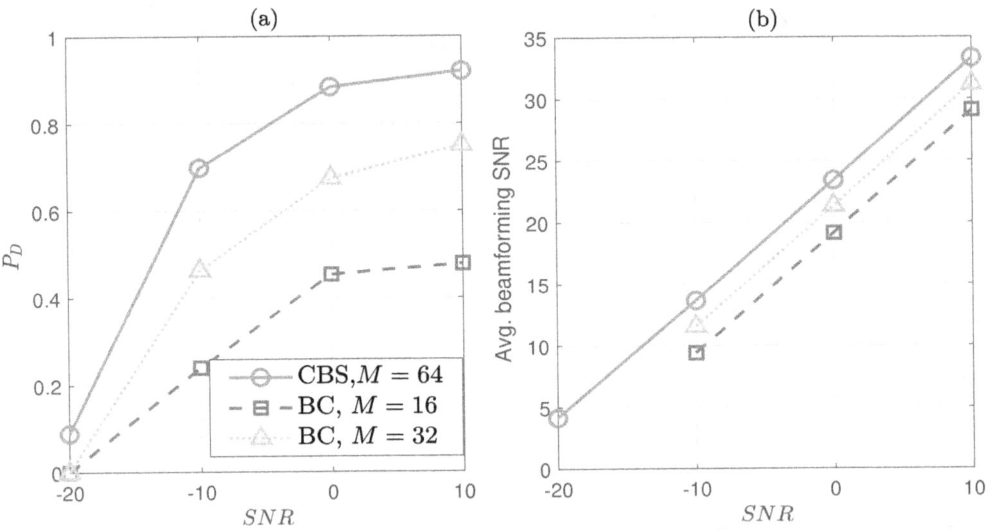

Figure 3.6: (a) Detect at least 1 active BS using sequence transmission. (b)Average beamforming SNR for the detected BS. Parameters are fixed as $N_A = 4$, $N_B = 100$ and $N_S = 11$ with ULA set up.

both plots, we notice that when SNR increases, the average beamforming SNR also increases for all methods. Further, the average beamforming SNR performance is the highest for CBS schemes. However, with an increase in α_1 or α_2, the resolution of the estimated AoA-AoD pair decreases, resulting in a decrease of beamforming gain and beamforming SNR. For Figure 3.6(b), $\mathbb{P}_D$ at $-20dB$ SNR is 0 and hence, at this point, the average beamforming SNR is not marked.

3.5.4   Effect of the number of BSs

In this section, we try to analyze CD performance in terms of the total number of BSs in the network (N_B). We plot $\mathbb{P}_D$ vs N_B in Figure 3.7. We observe that $\mathbb{P}_D$ decreases as N_B increases for all the schemes. As N_B increases, UE has to correlate with the SS of all these BSs for CD. Thus, the threshold to maintain the fixed $\mathbb{P}_F$ (0.01) also increases

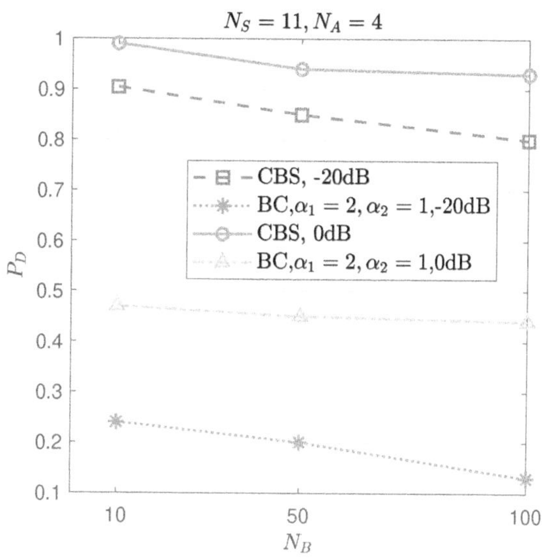

Figure 3.7: Impact of total number of BSs in the network on $\mathbb{P}_D$ with NYUSIM results.

resulting in the decrease of detection probability.

3.5.5 Analysis on CD failure & Time complexity

In Figure 3.8, we quantify the efficiency of CBS and BC methods, in terms of ($\mathbb{P}_{fail}$) and the expected number of attempts (N_{avg}) it takes for a typical UE to establish a reliable connection, within a total of N_{max} attempts. We assume *ideal channel* set-up with $N_A = N_B = 1, K = 3$ and $N_{max} = 10$. The results are averaged over 1000 channel realizations. Figure 3.8(a) plots $\mathbb{P}_{fail}$ vs receive SNR. We observe that $\mathbb{P}_{fail}$ decreases with increase in SNR. CBS technique has the least $\mathbb{P}_{fail}$ because of its high training overhead and high beam resolution. Figure 3.8(b) plots N_{avg} given successful detection of at least one active BS w.r.t SNR, thereby comparing the time complexity of the CD techniques. For both CBS and BC schemes, N_{avg} decreases with an increase in SNR. It is imperative to note that, the higher the $\mathbb{P}_{fail}$ value for a CD scheme, the

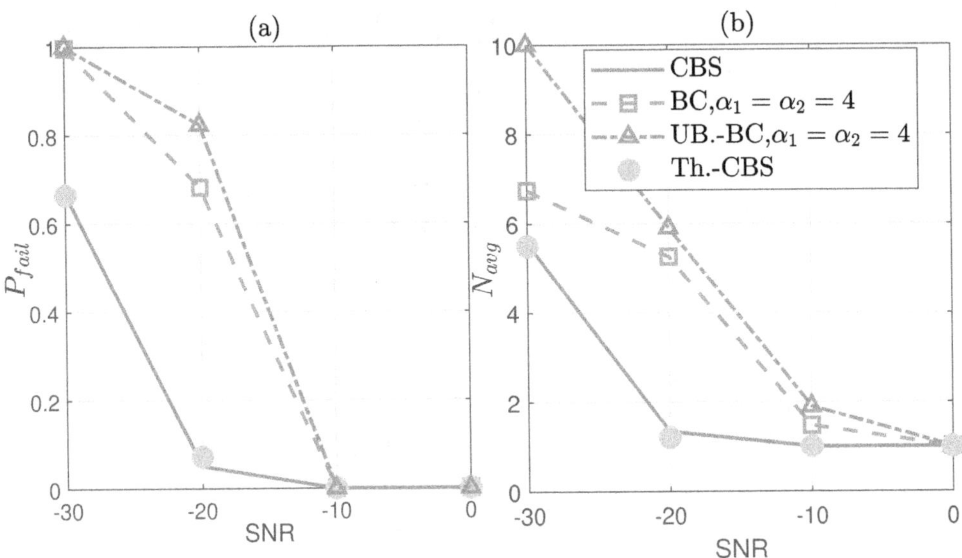

Figure 3.8: (a) CD failure probability. (b) Time complexity in terms of the expected number of average attempts. We set $N_A = 1$ and $N_{max} = 10$

UE needs more attempts to establish a link with at least one active BS using that CD scheme, i.e., N_{avg} will be larger.

3.6 SUMMARY

In this chapter, we first explained the beamforming training strategy for mmWave systems with multiple BSs for the hybrid beamforming architecture. We then mathematically formulated the cell discovery problem and addressed the physical layer implementation of beam-sweeping techniques for the cell discovery problem in millimeter wave communication systems. We considered beam sweep and beam combining schemes and presented the complete details of the transmit/receiver beamforming vectors in the training phase. We obtained analytical expressions of the detection probability, false alarm rate, average number of CD trials, and probability of CD failure of the schemes under ideal channel assumptions. We also discussed the beam sweeping scheme with synchronization sequences when multiple BSs are present in the network and derived the expression for the probability of detection when BSs transmit orthogonal synchronization sequences. We also presented simulation results using channels generated from NYUSIM for all the schemes.

CBS and BC schemes do not exploit the sparse nature of the mmWave channels. In subsequent Chapters, we model CD as a sparse recovery problem and develop new training schemes to accomplish fast cell discovery with better detection.

CHAPTER 4
Beamforming Training using Mutually Unbiased Bases

In Chapter 3, we discussed the beam sweeping based training schemes for CD in mmWave systems. Beam sweeping methods do not exploit the sparse nature of the mmWave channel. In this chapter, by exploiting the sparse nature of mmWave channels (Mo *et al.*, 2014; Lee *et al.*, 2016*b*), we formulate CD problem as a sparse signal recovery problem in compressive sensing (Candes and Wakin, 2008) and develop a new training scheme in which the beamforming vectors are designed based on mutually unbiased bases (MUB) from quantum information theory (Li and Ge, 2014). Unlike the design of random beamforming weights proposed in the literature, MUB based training scheme (MUBB) allows a deterministic way of constructing a large number of distinct beamforming vectors as the constituting MUB vectors can be easily generated over a Galois Ring as explained in (Li and Ge, 2014). We explicitly define the beamforming vectors to be used for CD for the hybrid beamforming architecture and characterize the mutual coherence parameter of the constructed sensing matrix. This sensing matrix needs to be available at the receiver algorithm for CD and hence contributes to the storage/memory requirement at the UE. Towards achieving fast CD, we also detail the procedure to do a coarser beam search using wider beams that provides a trade-off between the number of measurements and the recovery performance. We include design parameters to provide flexibility over the training duration and beam width of the MUB-based CD scheme and characterize the relation between mutual coherence and training overhead. We also derive analytical expression for the probability of detecting atleast a BS for MUB based training scheme under specialized channel conditions. We also explain how our proposed schemes can be incorporated with the 5G-NR framework for cell discovery. We explain how to extend the schemes for CD in wideband systems and show compatibility with other sparse recovery-based UE algorithms. Through simulation studies with practical mmWave channels generated using NYUSIM, we establish the superior performance of our MUB-based method over the conventional beam sweeping and random beamforming schemes in terms of detection probability and the post beamforming SNR with respect to the detected BS.

4.1 COMPRESSIVE SENSING MODEL

First, we write the received signal model in (3.5) according to the conventional sparse signal recovery framework. The techniques for cell discovery utilize the underlying sparse structure of $\mathbf{G}_i$ as mentioned in the system model in (2.4). From (3.5), by vectorizing the matrices (column-wise concatenation), with $\mathbf{y}_m = \mathrm{vec}(\mathbf{Y}_m), \mathbf{g}^{(i)} = \mathrm{vec}(\sqrt{\rho_i}\mathbf{G}_i)$ and $\mathbf{n}_m = \mathrm{vec}(\mathbf{N}_m)$, we have

$$\mathbf{y}_m = \sum_{i \in \mathcal{A}} x_m^{(i)} \mathbf{\Psi}^{(i)} \mathbf{g}^{(i)} + \mathbf{n}_m, \tag{4.1}$$

where $\mathbf{\Psi}^{(i)} = \bar{\mathbf{W}}_{t_i}^T \otimes \bar{\mathbf{W}}_r^*$. $\mathcal{A}$ denotes the set of unblocked BSs in the wireless network. Thus, $\mathbf{g}^{(i)} = \mathbf{0}$ for $i \notin \mathcal{A}$. Defining the *complete* channel vector $\mathbf{g} = \left[\mathbf{g}^{(1)T} \ \mathbf{g}^{(2)T} \ ... \ \left(\mathbf{g}^{(N_B)}\right)^T\right]^T$, we have $\mathbf{y}_m = \mathbf{\Psi}_m \mathbf{g} + \mathbf{n}_m$, where $\mathbf{\Psi}_m = \left[x_m^{(1)}\mathbf{\Psi}^{(1)}|x_m^{(2)}\mathbf{\Psi}^{(2)}|\cdots|x_m^{(N_B)}\mathbf{\Psi}^{(N_B)}\right]$. Now, concatenating the observations corresponding to all the symbols of the training signal $\bar{\mathbf{y}} = \left[\mathbf{y}_1^T \ \mathbf{y}_2^T \ ... \ \mathbf{y}_{N_S}^T\right]^T$, we have

$$\bar{\mathbf{y}} = \bar{\mathbf{\Psi}}\mathbf{g} + \bar{\mathbf{n}} \tag{4.2}$$

where $\bar{\boldsymbol{\Psi}} = \left[\mathbf{x}^{(1)} \otimes \boldsymbol{\Psi}^{(1)} | \mathbf{x}^{(2)} \otimes \boldsymbol{\Psi}^{(2)} | \cdots | \mathbf{x}^{(N_B)} \otimes \boldsymbol{\Psi}^{(N_B)}\right]$ and $\bar{\mathbf{n}} = [\mathbf{n}_1^T, ..., \mathbf{n}_{N_S}^T]$. $\mathbf{x}^{(i)}$ denote the synchronization signal of ith BS. $\bar{\boldsymbol{\Psi}}$ is termed as the sensing matrix in the sparse formulation. Since the number of active BS near UE is relatively small compared to the total number of BS in the network, g of length $N_t N_r N_B$ is a sparse signal. The goal is to recover the non-zero entries in g using the linear measurement model (4.2), which leads to the detection of (at-least one) active BS and the corresponding AoA-AoD pairs.

The detection of non-zero entries in g can be accomplished by correlating observation vector $\bar{\mathbf{y}}$ with each column of the sensing matrix $\bar{\boldsymbol{\Psi}}$ and comparing with a suitable threshold. We, therefore, implement the first iteration of the Stage wise Orthogonal Matching Pursuit (OMP) proposed in (Donoho et $al.$, 2012) as the detection algorithm at the UE. For $l \in \{1, \cdots, N_t N_r N_B\}$, we compute $z_l = [\bar{\boldsymbol{\Psi}}]_{:,l}^* \bar{\mathbf{y}}$ and declare that l^{th} entry in g is non-zero if

$$|z_l|^2 > \tau. \tag{4.3}$$

The threshold τ is selected as described in Section 3.3.1. Note that the $\bar{\boldsymbol{\Psi}}$ matrix must be stored at the UE for the above detector algorithm and hence contributes to the memory requirement at the UE.

Now, we analyze the detection performance of the above correlation-based energy detector. Let vector $\mathbf{g}_a$ of size T denote the *significant* non-zero valued entries in g and $\mathcal{T}$ denote the ordered support set of these significant entries. Let $\mathbf{g}_b$ denote the complementary set of insignificant entries (values close to zero) with the support set $\mathcal{T}^c$ (of size $N_t N_r N_B - T$). We can write

$$\bar{\mathbf{y}} = \bar{\mathbf{\Psi}}_{\mathcal{T}} \mathbf{g}_a + \bar{\mathbf{\Psi}}_{\mathcal{T}^c} \mathbf{g}_b + \bar{\mathbf{n}}, \tag{4.4}$$

where $\bar{\mathbf{\Psi}}_{\mathcal{T}}$ denotes the sub-matrix of $\bar{\mathbf{\Psi}}$ with the columns chosen from the set $\mathcal{T}$. Let us define the correlation vector corresponding to the active channel entries as $\mathbf{z}_a = \bar{\mathbf{\Psi}}_{\mathcal{T}}^* \bar{\mathbf{y}}$. We assume $\mathbf{g}_a$ and $\mathbf{g}_b$ are uncorrelated. Let $\mathbf{R}_{g_a}$ and $\mathbf{R}_{z_a}$ denote the covariance matrices of $\mathbf{g}_a$ and $\mathbf{z}_a$, respectively. For subsequent use, let $\sigma_{\min}^2$ denote the smallest eigenvalue of $\mathbf{R}_{g_a}$. The probability of detection ($\mathbb{P}_D$) for our detection rule is given by

$$\mathbb{P}_D = \mathbb{P}\left(\bigcup_{l \in \mathcal{T}} |z_l|^2 > \tau \right).$$

The *mutual coherence* parameter of the sensing matrix defined as,

$$\mu(\bar{\mathbf{\Psi}}) = \max_{l_1 \neq l_2} \frac{\left| [\bar{\mathbf{\Psi}}]_{:,l_1}^* [\bar{\mathbf{\Psi}}]_{:,l_2} \right|}{\left\| [\bar{\mathbf{\Psi}}]_{:,l_1} \right\|_2 \left\| [\bar{\mathbf{\Psi}}]_{:,l_2} \right\|_2}, \tag{4.5}$$

plays a significant role in the sparse signal recovery performance (Tropp, 2004) and is widely used as a measure of the ability of the receiver algorithm in identifying the exact sparse nature of the underlying signal. We also define smallest and largest column norms $c_{\min} = \min_l \left\| [\bar{\mathbf{\Psi}}]_{:,l} \right\|_2^2$ and $c_{\max} = \max_l \left\| [\bar{\mathbf{\Psi}}]_{:,l} \right\|_2^2$. $\mathbb{P}_D$ for the compressive sensing model is characterized below.

Theorem 6. *The probability of detection ($\mathbb{P}_D$) for the correlation-based energy detector* *is given by,*

$$\mathbb{P}_D \geq 1 - \prod_{k=1}^{|\mathcal{T}|} \left[1 - e^{-\frac{\tau|\mathcal{T}|}{\lambda_k}} \right] \tag{4.6}$$

$$\geq 1 - \left[1 - \exp\left(-\frac{\tau|\mathcal{T}|}{\sigma_{\min}^2 \bar{\mu}^2 + \sigma_n^2 \bar{\mu}} \right) \right]^{|\mathcal{T}|}, \tag{4.7}$$

where λ_k's are the eigenvalues of the covariance matrix $\mathbf{R}_{z_a}$ and $\bar{\mu} = \left(c_{\min} - \left(|\mathcal{T}| - 1 \right) c_{\max} \mu(\bar{\mathbf{\Psi}}) \right)$.

Proof. The correlation with active columns, $\mathbf{z}_a = \bar{\mathbf{\Psi}}_{\mathcal{T}}^* \bar{\mathbf{y}}$, is zero-mean Gaussian with covariance matrix,

$$\mathbf{R}_{z_a} = \left(\bar{\mathbf{\Psi}}_{\mathcal{T}}^* \bar{\mathbf{\Psi}}_{\mathcal{T}} \right) \mathbf{R}_{g_a} \left(\bar{\mathbf{\Psi}}_{\mathcal{T}}^* \bar{\mathbf{\Psi}}_{\mathcal{T}} \right)$$

$$+ \left(\bar{\mathbf{\Psi}}_{\mathcal{T}}^* \bar{\mathbf{\Psi}}_{\mathcal{T}^c} \right) \mathbf{R}_{g_b} \left(\bar{\mathbf{\Psi}}_{\mathcal{T}^c}^* \bar{\mathbf{\Psi}}_{\mathcal{T}} \right) + \sigma_n^2 \left(\bar{\mathbf{\Psi}}_{\mathcal{T}}^* \bar{\mathbf{\Psi}}_{\mathcal{T}} \right). \tag{4.8}$$

With the eigen decomposition $\mathbf{R}_{z_a} = \tilde{\mathbf{U}} \mathbf{\Lambda} \tilde{\mathbf{U}}^*$ and defining the unitary rotation $\tilde{\mathbf{z}}_a = \tilde{\mathbf{U}}^* \mathbf{z}_a$, we have $\tilde{\mathbf{z}}_a$ is zero mean Gaussian with diagonal covariance matrix $\mathbf{\Lambda}$. Now, the probability of detection is, $\mathbb{P}_D = \mathbb{P}\left(\bigcup_{k=1}^{|\mathcal{T}|} |[\mathbf{z}_a]_k|^2 > \tau \right) = 1 - \mathbb{P}\left(\bigcap_{k=1}^{|\mathcal{T}|} |[\mathbf{z}_a]_k|^2 \leq \tau \right)$. Under the event $\bigcap_{k=1}^{|\mathcal{T}|} |[\mathbf{z}_a]_k|^2 \leq \tau$, we have,

$$|[\tilde{\mathbf{z}}_a]_k|^2 = \left| [\tilde{\mathbf{U}}]_{:,k}^* \mathbf{z}_a \right|^2 \leq \sum_{i=1}^{|\mathcal{T}|} |[\tilde{\mathbf{U}}]_{i,k}|^2 \sum_{i=1}^{|\mathcal{T}|} |[\mathbf{z}_a]_i|^2 \leq \tau|\mathcal{T}| \|[\tilde{\mathbf{U}}]_{:,k}\|_2^2 = \tau|\mathcal{T}|, \forall k.$$

Thus, we conclude that the event $\left\{ \bigcap_{k=1}^{|\mathcal{T}|} |[\mathbf{z}_a]_k|^2 \leq \tau \right\}$ leads to the event $\left\{ \bigcap_{k=1}^{|\mathcal{T}|} |[\tilde{\mathbf{z}}_a]_k|^2 \leq \right.$

$\tau|\mathcal{T}|\Big\}$. Hence we get,

$$\mathbb{P}\left(\bigcap_{k=1}^{|\mathcal{T}|} |[\mathbf{z_a}]_k|^2 \leq \tau\right) \leq \mathbb{P}\left(\bigcap_{k=1}^{|\mathcal{T}|} |[\tilde{\mathbf{z}}_a]_k|^2 \leq \tau|\mathcal{T}|\right).$$

The entries $\left\{|[\tilde{\mathbf{z}}_a]_k|^2\right\}_{k=1}^{|\mathcal{T}|}$ are independent exponential random variables with parameters $\frac{1}{\lambda_k} = \frac{1}{[\mathbf{\Lambda}]_{k,k}}$, we get, $\mathbb{P}_D \geq 1 - \prod_{k=1}^{|\mathcal{T}|}\left[1 - e^{-\frac{\tau|\mathcal{T}|}{\lambda_k}}\right]$.

Now, we derive the lower bound on $\mathbb{P}_D$, by lower bounding the eigenvalue of $\mathbf{R}_{z_a}$. In the positive definite sense, we have $\mathbf{R}_{z_a} \geq \mathbf{C}_{\min} = \sigma_{\min}^2 \mathbf{T}^2 + \sigma_n^2 \mathbf{T}$, where $\mathbf{T} = \bar{\mathbf{\Psi}}_{\mathcal{T}}^* \bar{\mathbf{\Psi}}_{\mathcal{T}}$ and $\sigma_{\min}^2$ is the smallest eigenvalue of $\mathbf{R}_{g_a}$. Hence, each eigenvalue λ_k of $\mathbf{R}_{z_a}$ will be greater than the smallest eigenvalue of $\mathbf{C}_{\min}$. If β is an eigenvalue of $\mathbf{T}$ with some eigenvector, then $\mathbf{C}_{\min}$ will have the same eigenvector with corresponding eigenvalue being $\sigma_{\min}^2\beta^2 + \sigma_n^2\beta$. Using Gershgorin's disk theorem (Horn and Johnson, 2012), every eigenvalue of $\mathbf{T}$ can be lower bounded as $\beta \geq \bar{\mu} = c_{\min} - (|\mathcal{T}| - 1)c_{\max}\mu(\bar{\mathbf{\Psi}})$. This implies that $\lambda_k \geq \sigma_{\min}^2\bar{\mu}^2 + \sigma_n^2\bar{\mu}$ and the lower bound in (4.7) follows. $\qquad\square$

From the lower bound expression of $\mathbb{P}_D$ in (4.7), smaller the value of $\mu(\bar{\mathbf{\Psi}})$, larger will be $\bar{\mu}$ and hence a larger $\mathbb{P}_D$. That is, the lesser correlation between the columns of $\bar{\mathbf{\Psi}}$ results in better recovery performance. Hence, CD performance depends on the design of $\bar{\mathbf{\Psi}}$. In the next section, we develop MUB based training scheme which can result in small μ for $\bar{\mathbf{\Psi}}$.

4.2   MUTUALLY UNBIASED BASES BASED BEAMFORMING:

In this section we design the beamforming matrices $\bar{\mathbf{W}}_r$ and $\bar{\mathbf{W}}_{t_i}, i = 1, \cdots, N_B$, in (3.5) using MUB matrices, such that the resulting sensing matrix $\bar{\mathbf{\Psi}}$ in (4.2) has low mutual coherence. MUBs were originally used in quantum information theory for quantum state determination, however later found applications in quantum key distribution, quantum state construction, quantum error correction codes etc.

A set of $d \times d$ matrices $\mathbf{B}_1, \mathbf{B}_2, ..., \mathbf{B}_d$ are said to be mutually unbiased bases, if, $\mathbf{B}_l^* \mathbf{B}_l = \mathbf{I}_d$, $\forall l = 1, ..., d$, and $\left| [\mathbf{B}_{i_1}]_{:,l}^* [\mathbf{B}_{i_2}]_{:,k} \right| = \frac{1}{\sqrt{d}}$, $\forall i_1 \neq i_2; l, k = 1, ..., d.$. Constructions for MUB matrices exist when $d = p^n$, where p is a prime number and n is a non-negative integer (Li and Ge, 2014; Aditi $et\ al.$, 2020).

Based on the hardware set-up, UPAs support two different antenna configurations, namely separable and non-separable designs (Van Trees, Harry L, 2004; Kummer, 1992). Non-separable antenna configuration allows control of the antenna weights assigned to each antenna element, and the beamforming vector design is similar to the ULA design procedure. In separable antenna configuration, for example, at the BS, the $N_t \times 1$ beamforming vector $\mathbf{w}_t$ needs to be expressed as Kronecker product $\mathbf{w}_t = \mathbf{w}_{t_a} \otimes \mathbf{w}_{t_e}$ where $\mathbf{w}_{t_a}$ is beamforming vector of size $N_{t_1} \times 1$ along azimuth direction and $\mathbf{w}_{t_e}$ is beamforming vector of size $N_{t_2} \times 1$ along elevation direction. We discuss the MUB based beamforming (MUBB) scheme for both of these configurations below.

Though MUB matrices exist for dimensions of any prime power, we illustrate our transmit beamforming matrix design assuming that N_{t_1}, N_{t_2} are powers of 2. In this case, it is worth noting that the entries in all the MUB matrices belong to the appropriately scaled version of the set $\{1, -1, j, -j\}$. We introduce a *reduction* parameter u, which sets the number of transmit beamforming weights used in the training phase as $Q = \frac{N_t}{2^u}$. Clearly, as u increases, the duration of the training phase decreases. We will later see the impact of u on the mutual coherence of the sensing matrix $\bar{\boldsymbol{\Psi}}$. For both separable and non-separable configurations, we will construct $I_{\max} = \frac{N_t}{2^{2u}}$ distinct beamforming weight matrices $\bar{\mathbf{W}}_{t_{\bar{i}}}$ of size $N_t \times \frac{N_t}{2^u}$ for $\bar{i} \in \{1, \cdots, I_{\max}\}$. These beamforming matrices are assigned among N_B BSs based on simple modulo operation, such that BS with identity i gets the beamforming matrix $\bar{\mathbf{W}}_{t_{\bar{i}}}$, where $\bar{i} = (i \mod I_{\max}) + 1$. For convenience, we use i instead of $\bar{i}$ in describing the beamforming weights, with the understanding that there is an underlying modulo operation involved.

First, we address the transmit beamforming design for non-separable configuration, where we directly construct $N_t \times 1$ beamforming vectors. Now, $\bar{\mathbf{W}}_{t_i}$ are constructed by concatenating MUB matrices of dimension $\frac{N_t}{2^u}$ as follows. Let $\left\{ \mathbf{M}_a \right\}_{a=1}^{\frac{N_t}{2^u}}$ be a collection of $\frac{N_t}{2^u} \times \frac{N_t}{2^u}$ unitary MUB matrices. We concatenate 2^u numbers of unique MUB matrices and set $\bar{\mathbf{W}}_{t_i} = \mathbf{M}^{(i)^T}$ where

$$\mathbf{M}^{(i)} = \frac{1}{\sqrt{2^u}} \left[\mathbf{M}_{(i-1)2^u+1} \middle| \mathbf{M}_{(i-1)2^u+2} \middle| \dots \middle| \mathbf{M}_{i2^u} \right]. \tag{4.9}$$

Note that the scaling factor $\frac{1}{\sqrt{2^u}}$ in the above construction ensures that the resulting transmit beamforming weights are of unit norm. Since each beamforming matrix $\mathbf{W}_{t_i}$ requires 2^u distinct MUB matrices, the number of distinct beamforming weight matrices possible equals $I_{\max} = \frac{N_t}{2^{2u}}$.

Now, we describe the transmit beamforming design for the separable configuration. Say we use a reduction factor of u_1 along the azimuth direction and a reduction factor of u_2 along the elevation direction. The net reduction factor is given by $u = u_1 + u_2$. The construction of beamforming weights along azimuth and elevation resembles the non-separable MUB construction (4.9).

Specifically, let $\tilde{\mathcal{M}} = \left\{ \tilde{\mathbf{M}}_b \right\}_{b=1}^{\frac{N_{t_1}}{2^{u_1}}}$ and $\hat{\mathcal{M}} = \left\{ \hat{\mathbf{M}}_c \right\}_{c=1}^{\frac{N_{t_2}}{2^{u_2}}}$ be the sets of MUB matrices of dimensions $\frac{N_{t_1}}{2^{u_1}}$ and $\frac{N_{t_2}}{2^{u_2}}$ respectively. For $i_k \in \{1, \cdots, \frac{N_{t_1}}{2^{2u_1}}\}$, and $i_l \in \{1, \cdots, \frac{N_{t_2}}{2^{2u_2}}\}$, we concatenate MUB matrices as

$$\tilde{\mathbf{M}}^{(i_k)} = \frac{1}{\sqrt{2^{u_1}}} \left[\tilde{\mathbf{M}}_{(i_k-1)2^{u_1}+1} \middle| \tilde{\mathbf{M}}_{(i_k-1)2^{u_1}+2} \middle| \cdots \middle| \tilde{\mathbf{M}}_{i_k 2^{u_1}} \right], \qquad (4.10)$$

$$\hat{\mathbf{M}}^{(i_l)} = \frac{1}{\sqrt{2^{u_2}}} \left[\hat{\mathbf{M}}_{(i_l-1)2^{u_2}+1} \middle| \hat{\mathbf{M}}_{(i_l-1)2^{u_2}+2} \middle| \cdots \middle| \tilde{\mathbf{M}}_{i_l 2^{u_2}} \right], \qquad (4.11)$$

and construct the beamforming weight matrices as

$$\bar{\mathbf{W}}_{t_i}^T = \mathbf{M}^{(i)} = \tilde{\mathbf{M}}^{(i_k)} \otimes \hat{\mathbf{M}}^{(i_l)}. \qquad (4.12)$$

Since there are $\frac{N_{t_1}}{2^{2u_1}}$ matrices for azimuth and $\frac{N_{t_2}}{2^{2u_2}}$ matrices for elevation directions, we have a total of $\frac{N_{t_1} N_{t_2}}{2^{2(u_1+u_2)}}$ distinct Kronecker products, resulting in $\frac{N_t}{2^{2u}}$ distinct beamforming matrices. Note that the conditions $2^{2u_1} \leq N_{t_1}$ and $2^{2u_2} \leq N_{t_2}$ must be satisfied for the above construction methodology.

We can do similar construction using MUB matrices to design the beamforming matrix at UE. Since the antenna dimensions at the UE are typically small, we do not need any reduction parameter at the receive side beamforming. We can set $\bar{\mathbf{W}}_r = \mathbf{M}^*$ where $\mathbf{M}$ is an $N_r \times N_r$ unitary matrix for non-separable configuration, and $\mathbf{M} = \mathbf{M}_{r_1} \otimes \mathbf{M}_{r_2}$ for separable configuration with $\mathbf{M}_{r_1}$ and $\mathbf{M}_{r_2}$ being unitary matrices of dimension N_{r_1} and N_{r_2} respectively.

In this case, we get $P = N_r$. Now, the overall training duration for the MUBB design is $\frac{N_t N_r N_S}{2^u}$, with $u = u_1 + u_2$ for the separable configuration.

Note that the above construction ensures that both the transmit and receive beamforming vectors to be used during every pilot transmission are of unit norm. Also, the beamforming vectors are constructed in a deterministic way using the column vectors of MUB matrices. Further, the sensing matrix $\mathbf{\Psi}^{(i)}$ in (4.1) can be written as, $\mathbf{\Psi}^{(i)} = \mathbf{M}^{(i)} \otimes \mathbf{M}$. Hence, the sensing matrix $\bar{\mathbf{\Psi}}$ from (4.2) is horizontal concatenation blocks $\bar{\mathbf{\Psi}}^{(i)} = \mathbf{x}^{(i)} \otimes [\mathbf{M}^{(i)} \otimes \mathbf{M}]$. The mutual coherence parameter μ of the resulting sensing matrix $\bar{\mathbf{\Psi}}$ depends on the MUB design and also on the correlation among the synchronization signals (3.1).

Theorem 7. *For the non-separable design, we have*

$$
\mu(\bar{\mathbf{\Psi}}) = \begin{cases} \sqrt{\dfrac{2^u}{N_t}}, & \textit{if } N_B \leq \mathcal{N}_{\max}, \\[2ex] \max\left(\sqrt{\dfrac{2^u}{N_t}}, \dfrac{\varsigma}{N_S} \right), & \textit{if } N_B > \mathcal{N}_{\max}. \end{cases}
$$

For the separable design, we have

$$
\mu(\bar{\mathbf{\Psi}}) = \begin{cases} \max\left(\sqrt{\frac{2^{u_1}}{N_{t_1}}}, \sqrt{\frac{2^{u_2}}{N_{t_2}}}\right), & \text{if } N_B \leq \mathcal{N}_{\max}, \\ \max\left(\sqrt{\frac{2^{u_1}}{N_{t_1}}}, \sqrt{\frac{2^{u_2}}{N_{t_2}}}, \frac{\zeta}{N_S}\right), & \text{if } N_B > \mathcal{N}_{\max}. \end{cases}
$$

Proof. We describe the proof for the separable case. The result for the non-separable case can be obtained similarly. Note that $\bar{\mathbf{\Psi}}$ is obtained by concatenating matrices $\bar{\mathbf{\Psi}}^{(i)} = \mathbf{x}^{(i)} \otimes [\mathbf{M}^{(i)} \otimes \mathbf{M}]$ corresponding to each base station i. We note that $\mathbf{M}^{(i)}$ in (4.12) has unit norm rows (since its transpose gives the beamforming weights, which are unit norm) and the column norms are equal to $\frac{1}{\sqrt{2^{u_1+u_2}}}$. Since $\mathbf{M}$ is unitary and the column norm of $\mathbf{x}^{(i)}$ is $\sqrt{N_S}$, all the columns of $\bar{\mathbf{\Psi}}^{(i)}$ have norm equal to $\sqrt{\frac{N_S}{2^{u_1+u_2}}}$, for all i. The coherence $\mu(\bar{\mathbf{\Psi}})$ depends on the entries of

$$
\bar{\mathbf{\Psi}}^{(i)*}\bar{\mathbf{\Psi}}^{(j)} = \mathbf{x}^{(i)*}\mathbf{x}^{(j)}\left[\mathbf{M}^{(i)*}\mathbf{M}^{(j)} \otimes \mathbf{I}_{N_r}\right], \forall i, j. \tag{4.13}
$$

Considering the case when $i = j$, we define ρ_i as the maximum cross-correlation/inner-product between the columns of $\bar{\mathbf{\Psi}}^{(i)}$ which is given by the maximum magnitude of the off-diagonal entries in $\bar{\mathbf{\Psi}}^{(i)*}\bar{\mathbf{\Psi}}^{(i)} = N_S\left[\mathbf{M}^{(i)*}\mathbf{M}^{(i)} \otimes \mathbf{I}_{N_r}\right]$. From (4.1) and (4.2), we can infer that a smaller value of ρ_i implies better ability at the receiver to distinguish between the different FFT bins of the beamspace matrix $\mathbf{G}_i$, using the given observations. Based on the design constructions (4.10),(4.11),(4.12), the non-zero off diagonal entries of $\mathbf{M}^{(i)*}\mathbf{M}^{(i)}$ are of the form $\frac{1}{2^{u_1+u_2}}[\tilde{\mathbf{M}}_b \otimes \hat{\mathbf{M}}_c]^*[\tilde{\mathbf{M}}_{\bar{b}} \otimes \hat{\mathbf{M}}_{\bar{c}}]$.

Now,

$$[\tilde{\mathbf{M}}_b \otimes \hat{\mathbf{M}}_c]^*[\tilde{\mathbf{M}}_{\bar{b}} \otimes \hat{\mathbf{M}}_{\bar{c}}] = \begin{cases} \dfrac{\mathbf{I}_{N_{t_1}}}{2^{u_1}} \otimes \sqrt{\dfrac{2^{u_2}}{N_{t_2}}}\grave{\mathbf{Q}}_1 & \text{if } b = \bar{b}, \\[3mm] \sqrt{\dfrac{2^{u_1}}{N_{t_1}}}\grave{\mathbf{Q}}_2 \otimes \dfrac{\mathbf{I}_{N_{t_2}}}{2^{u_2}} & \text{if } c = \bar{c}, \end{cases} \tag{4.14}$$

where $\grave{\mathbf{Q}}_1$ and $\grave{\mathbf{Q}}_2$ are matrices with all entries having unit magnitude. Hence $\rho_i = \frac{N_S}{2^{u_1+u_2}} \max\left\{ \sqrt{\frac{1}{2^{u_2}N_{t_1}}}, \sqrt{\frac{1}{2^{u_1}N_{t_2}}} \right\}$.

Now, for the case when $i \neq j$, we have two situations. 1) The beamforming matrices are distinct, that is, $\mathbf{M}^{(i)} \neq \mathbf{M}^{(j)}$. When $N_B \leq \mathcal{N}_{\max}$, we are guaranteed of this situation. 2) The beamforming matrices are identical, that is, $\mathbf{M}^{(i)} = \mathbf{M}^{(j)}$. When $N_B > \mathcal{N}_{\max}$, this situation is inevitable, for some values of i and j. Considering the first situation, let $\rho_{1,i,j}$ denote the maximum of the magnitude of the entries in

$$\bar{\mathbf{\Psi}}^{(i)*}\bar{\mathbf{\Psi}}^{(j)} = \mathbf{x}^{(i)*}\mathbf{x}^{(j)}\left[\mathbf{M}^{(i)*}\mathbf{M}^{(j)} \otimes \mathbf{I}_{N_r}\right].$$ Again, based on the design construction, the entries of $\mathbf{M}^{(i)*}\mathbf{M}^{(j)}$ will be of the form described in (4.14). Using (3.1), we have $\rho_{1,i,j} = \frac{\zeta}{2^{u_1+u_2}} \max\left\{ \sqrt{\frac{1}{2^{u_2}N_{t_1}}}, \sqrt{\frac{1}{2^{u_1}N_{t_2}}} \right\}$. Now, considering the second situation, let $\rho_{2,i,j}$ denote the maximum of the magnitude of the entries in $\mathbf{x}^{(i)*}\mathbf{x}^{(j)}\left[\mathbf{M}^{(i)*}\mathbf{M}^{(i)} \otimes \mathbf{I}_{N_r}\right]$. Since square of the norm of all the columns of $\mathbf{M}^{(i)}$ are identical to $\frac{1}{2^{u_1+u_2}}$, we have $\rho_{2,i,j} = \frac{\zeta}{2^{u_1+u_2}}$. Since the mutual coherence is the maximum correlation normalized by the column norms, we have the results as given below.

$$\mu(\bar{\mathbf{\Psi}}) = \begin{cases} \dfrac{2^{u_1+u_2}}{N_S} \max(\rho_i, \rho_{1,i,j}), & \text{if } N_B \leq \mathcal{N}_{\max}, \\[3mm] \dfrac{2^{u_1+u_2}}{N_S} \max(\rho_i, \rho_{2,i,j}), & \text{if } N_B > \mathcal{N}_{\max}, \end{cases}$$

$\square$

We note that the mutual coherence of MUB design is inversely proportional to the antenna dimension at the transmitter. For large antenna arrays at the BS, we get small values for $\mu(\bar{\Psi})$. As the design parameters u or (u_1, u_2) increase, the training duration decreases, and the mutual coherence $\mu(\bar{\Psi})$ correspondingly increases, neatly characterizing the trade-off between overhead and performance. Similarly, small normalized cross-correlation among the synchronization signals $\frac{\zeta}{N_S}$ helps in reducing the coherence of the sensing matrix. More correlation between the sequences results in higher $\mu(\bar{\Psi})$, which in turn affects the correct identification of BS. Note that I_{max} is large when antenna dimensions are big. Thus MUBB provides a simple deterministic way of constructing $I_{\max}$ distinct transmit beamforming matrices that can be assigned to different BSs.

4.3   TRAINING USING WIDER BEAMS WITH MUBB.

Note that the MUBB design in Section 4.2, aims at recovering the non-zero entries in fine resolution beamspace matrices $\mathbf{G}_i$ which have $N_t N_r$ entries. When we reduce the number of measurements by increasing the parameter u, the mutual coherence increases, and the recovery performance degrades. To address this issue, we develop a scheme denoted as MUBB^w, which combines the MUBB design with the coarse/wider beams from Section 3.3.2. Let $\mathbf{S}_{N_t,\alpha}$ denote the transmit beam combining matrix from Section 3.3.2, which groups α bins/beams in the transmit direction. Similarly, let $\mathbf{S}_{N_r,\beta}$ denote the receive beam combining matrix. As noted in Section 3.3.2, we can also control the grouping of bins along azimuth and elevation separately. Now, we set the beamforming weight matrices $\bar{\mathbf{W}}_{t_i} = \mathbf{S}_{N_t,\alpha} \bar{\mathbf{W}}_{t_i}^w$ and $\bar{\mathbf{W}}_r = \mathbf{S}_{N_t,\beta} \bar{\mathbf{W}}_r^w$, where $\bar{\mathbf{W}}_{t_i}^w$ (of size $\frac{N_t}{\alpha} \times Q$) and $\bar{\mathbf{W}}_r^w$ (of size $\frac{N_r}{\beta} \times P$) are to be designed suitably. Under this set-up, using (3.5) and (3.17), we have

$$\mathbf{Y}_m = \sum_{i \in \mathcal{A}} \sqrt{\rho_i} \bar{\mathbf{W}}_r^{w^*} \mathbf{G}_i^w \bar{\mathbf{W}}_{t_i}^w x_m^{(i)} + \mathbf{N}_m. \tag{4.15}$$

In the above model, we can design $\bar{\mathbf{W}}_{t_i}^w$ and $\bar{\mathbf{W}}_r^w$ to recover the coarse lower resolution beamspace matrix $\mathbf{G}_i^w$. The MUBB designs discussed in Section 4.2 can be carried forward here, albeit for a smaller size $\frac{N_r}{\beta} \times \frac{N_t}{\alpha}$ beamspace matrix. Since the beamspace matrix is smaller, we can get a good recovery performance with smaller values of P and Q when compared to the fine-resolution beamspace matrix recovery. Another outcome is that we can have a larger value of $I_{\max}$, meaning we get more distinct beamforming weight matrices which can be assigned among different BS. We also note that we can replace $\mathbf{S}_{N_t,\alpha}$ with the combining matrix in (3.20), which enables flexibility in the grouping of α_1 bins along azimuth and α_2 bins along elevation directions.

4.4 5G NR FRAMEWORK FOR CELL DISCOVERY

In this section, we briefly explain the 5G-NR framework for cell discovery. Millimeter-wave physical layer initial access/cell discovery in 5G-NR cellular network is carried out using two functional blocks of the 5G-NR frame, namely synchronization signal burst (SS) and channel state information reference signal (CSI-RS) (Han and Danijela, 2019).

Each frame contains one SS burst set with a maximum of up to 64 SS blocks, and a unique transmit/receive beam pair is used by BS and UE for each SS block as shown

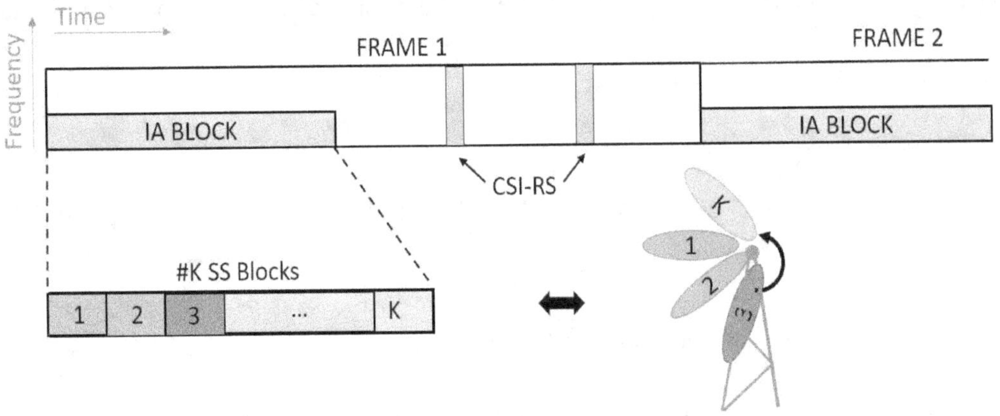

Figure 4.1: 5G frame structure for initial access. K= $PQ \leq 64$

in Figure 4.1. This is similar to our model in (3.2) with $PQ \leq 64$. UE carries out the cell discovery and coarse channel AoA-AoD estimation using SS signal. Specific UEs with high beamforming gain requirements use CSI-RS to refine the angular resolution by fine-tuning with the narrow beams within the identified beam sector. An SS block signal consists of a primary synchronization signal (PSS), physical broadcast channel information, and secondary synchronization signal (SSS). In 5G NR, M-sequences of length 128 are used for PSS and SSS signals which facilitate cell identification and synchronization. There are 3 PSS and 336 SSS signals, generating a total of 1008 unique cell identities. In simulations, we consider 5G-NR SSS sequences as the synchronization signals and compare the existing beamforming training schemes with the proposed MUBB schemes.

The 5G NR standard allows for various system bandwidths and OFDM subcarrier spacings. The possible system bandwidth values are 50 MHz, 100 MHz, 200 MHz and 400 MHz, and the possible subcarrier spacings are 15 kHz, 30 kHz, 60 kHz, 120 kHz and 480 kHz (3GPP TS 38.300, 2017). Synchronization signals such as PSS and

SSS occupy only 128 subcarriers. With a nominal subcarrier spacing of 60 kHz, the bandwidth occupied by the SS will only be 7.5 MHz, even if the system bandwidth is large, say, 100 MHz. Also, due to huge propagation losses, the RMS delay spread of the mm wave channels is typically small. If the RMS delay spread is of the order of tens of nano seconds (Zhang *et al.*, 2015), the coherence bandwidth of the channel will be larger than the PSS/SSS bandwidth. Hence, our frequency flat model for the synchronizations signals in (3.2) is valid in practical scenarios of interest.

4.5 EXTENSION OF CD FRAMEWORK TO WIDEBAND SYSTEMS

Our work so far has focused on cell discovery for narrowband systems with frequency flat channels. In the scenarios where the subcarrier spacing is large (say, 240 kHz) and/or the mm wave channels have large delay spreads (of the order of hundreds of nano seconds), the synchronization signals experience frequency selective fading. In this frequency selective wideband model, the sparsity needs to be modelled in the angle-delay domain (Venugopal *et al.*, 2017*a*; Chen *et al.*, 2019*a*). In this section, we discuss how our MUBB training designs for cell discovery can be adopted to wideband mm wave systems with suitable changes in the receiver processing.

For simplicity, we begin with a single BS scenario to explain the wideband model and later extend to multiple BSs. Hence we discard the superscript i and denote the channel matrix between the single BS and UE as $\mathbf{H}$. In accordance with the 5G NR framework explained in Section 4.4, the BS and UE fix a particular beamforming vector pair during an SS burst. BS then transmits its synchronization sequence. Consider a block transmission of block length N_S and a cyclic prefix (CP) of N_{cp} samples. Then, the received samples (3.2) for the wideband system model with N_c paths can be written as (Han and Danijela, 2019; Venugopal *et al.*, 2017*b*),

$$y_m(l) = \sum_{d=0}^{N_c-1} \sqrt{\rho}\mathbf{w}_r^{(m)*}\mathbf{H}(d)\mathbf{w}_t^{(m)}x_m(l-d)$$

$$+ \underbrace{\mathbf{w}_r^{(m)*}\mathbf{n}_m}_{n_m(l)}, \quad l = 1, ..., N_S. \tag{4.16}$$

Here, $y_m(l)$ denotes the lth received symbol for m^{th} SS block when m^{th} beamforming vectors $\mathbf{w}_t^{(m)}$ and $\mathbf{w}_r^{(m)}$ are used at the BS and the UE, respectively. Let us defind the transmit vector with CP $\mathbf{x} = [x(N_S - N_{cp} + 1), ..., x(N_S), x(1), x(2), \cdots, x(N_S)]^T$, the channel matrix $\mathbf{H} = [\mathbf{H}(0)^T, \mathbf{H}(1)^T, \cdots, \mathbf{H}(N_c - 1)^T]$, and the the column-wise concatenations $\mathbf{h} = \text{vec}(\mathbf{H})$ and $\mathbf{h}(d) = \text{vec}(\mathbf{H}(d))$. Now, (4.16) can be rearranged as,

$$y_m(l) = \sum_{d=0}^{N_c-1} \left[x_m(l-d)\mathbf{w}_t^{(m)T} \otimes \mathbf{w}_r^{(m)*} \right] \sqrt{\rho}\mathbf{h}(d) + n_m(l), \tag{4.17}$$

$$= \left[x_m(l)\mathbf{w}_t^{(m)T} \otimes \mathbf{w}_r^{(m)*}, \cdots, \right.$$

$$\left. x_m(l - N_c + 1)\mathbf{w}_t^{(m)T} \otimes \mathbf{w}_r^{(m)*} \right] \sqrt{\rho}\mathbf{h} + n_m(l). \tag{4.18}$$

The Saleh-Valenzuela wideband channel model for the discrete-time delay d is given by (Han and Danijela, 2019; Chen *et al.*, 2019*b*),

$$\mathbf{H}(d) = \sum_{k=1}^{K} \alpha_k p(dT_s - \tau_k)\mathbf{a}_{r_k}(\theta_k^r, \phi_k^r)\mathbf{a}_{t_k}(\theta_k^t, \phi_k^t)^*, \tag{4.19}$$

where $d = 0, ..., N_c - 1$. Note that the above channel model is similar to the narrowband channel model given in (2.3). The maximum value of d depends on the delay spread which is set as N_c and CP length is selected such that $N_{cp} > N_c$. The bandlimited pulse shaping filter response in the time domain is given by $p(t)$. The antenna response vectors $\mathbf{a}_{t_k}$ and $\mathbf{a}_{r_k}$ for UPA and ULA structures are given in Section 2.4. The sparse beamspace matrix for $\mathbf{H}(d)$ can be obtained using the transformation explained in (2.4) as, $\mathbf{G}(d) = \bar{\mathbf{F}}^*_{N_r} \mathbf{H}(d) \bar{\mathbf{F}}_{N_t}$. Considering all the delay taps, the beamspace channel of the frequency selective channel can be written as $\mathbf{G} = [\mathbf{G}(0), \mathbf{G}(1), .., \mathbf{G}(N_c - 1)]$. Now, by grouping the channel and the transmit power together, the unknown vector can be written as $\mathbf{g} = \sqrt{\rho}\mathrm{vec}(\mathbf{G})$.

By defining beamforming vectors as $\tilde{\mathbf{w}}_t^{(m)} = \bar{\mathbf{F}}_{N_t} \mathbf{w}_t^{(m)}$ and $\tilde{\mathbf{w}}_r^{(m)} = \bar{\mathbf{F}}_{N_r} \mathbf{w}_r^{(m)}$, (4.18) can be written as

$$
\begin{aligned}
y_m[l] &= \left[x_m(l)\tilde{\mathbf{w}}_t^{(m)T} \otimes \tilde{\mathbf{w}}_r^{(m)*}, \cdots, \right. \\
&\qquad \left. x_m(l - N_c + 1)\mathbf{w}_{\tilde{t}}^{(m)T} \otimes \tilde{\mathbf{w}}_r^{(m)*} \right] \mathbf{g} + n_m(l) \\
&= \Psi_m^l \mathbf{g} + n_m(l).
\end{aligned}
\tag{4.20}
$$

Now by appending all the received symbols corresponding to m^{th} beam-pair, the above equation can be written as $\mathbf{y}_m = \Psi_m \mathbf{g} + \mathbf{n}_m$ where $\mathbf{y}_m = [y_m[1], y_m[2], ..., y_m[N_S]]^T$, $\mathbf{n}_m = [n_m[1], ..., n_m[N_S]]^T$, and l^{th} row of Ψ_m is Ψ_m^l. Taking into account the entire training duration by using M training beams, the final system model can be written as

$$
\bar{\mathbf{y}} - \bar{\Psi}\mathbf{g} + \bar{\mathbf{n}},
\tag{4.21}
$$

with $\bar{\mathbf{y}} = [\mathbf{y}_1^T, \mathbf{y}_2^T, ..., \mathbf{y}_M^T]$ and $\bar{\mathbf{n}} = [\mathbf{n}_1^T, \mathbf{n}_2^T, ..., \mathbf{n}_M^T]$. The sensing matrix $\bar{\boldsymbol{\Psi}}$ is obtained by concatenating $\boldsymbol{\Psi}_m$, for $m = 1$ to M, one below the other. We can set the beamforming weights $\tilde{\mathbf{w}}_t^{(m)}$ and $\tilde{\mathbf{w}}_r^{(m)}$ as per the MUBB designs given in Section 4.2. Since the resulting wideband model (4.21) has been written in a form which resembles the previous model (4.2), the detectors given for the previous model (4.2) can be straightforwardly extended for the wideband model as well. In this case, the detector tries to find the locations of the strongest entries in the beamspace matrix $\mathbf{G}(d)$ corresponding to the strogest multipath component in the delay domain $d \in \{0, \cdots, N_c - 1\}$.

The system model for multiple BS conditions can be obtained by the straightforward extension of the single BS model. By using index i to represent the ith BS, the received signal from the ith BS can be written as $\bar{\boldsymbol{\Psi}}^{(i)}\mathbf{g}^{(i)}$. Hence, the total received signal at the UE becomes,

$$
\begin{aligned}
\bar{\mathbf{y}} &= \sum_i^{N_B} \bar{\boldsymbol{\Psi}}^{(i)}\mathbf{g}^{(i)} + \bar{\mathbf{n}} \\
&= \underbrace{\left[\bar{\boldsymbol{\Psi}}^{(1)}|\bar{\boldsymbol{\Psi}}^{(2)}|...|\bar{\boldsymbol{\Psi}}^{(N_B)}\right]}_{\bar{\boldsymbol{\Psi}}} \mathbf{g} + \bar{\mathbf{n}} \\
&= \bar{\boldsymbol{\Psi}}\mathbf{g} + \bar{\mathbf{n}},
\end{aligned}
\tag{4.22}
$$

where $\mathbf{g}$ is the unknown channel vector, $\mathbf{g}^T = \left[\mathbf{g}^{(1)T}, ..., \mathbf{g}^{(N_B)T}\right]$. The dimension of the $\mathbf{g}$ vector is $N_t N_r N_c N_B$ when N_B base stations are present in the network. Hence, finding the location of a significant entry in $\mathbf{g}$ vector maps to the identification of the base station, the delay index of the channel of the BS, and the corresponding transmit-receive beam pair for an accessible path. Wideband-specific UE algorithms, specifically designed considering the structure of the resulting sensing matrix might reduce the complexity of the scheme manifold. Further, the MUBB training scheme using widened beams discussed in Section 4.3 can be extended for CD in wideband systems for reducing the complexity of the UE algorithm

When large antenna arrays are used or when the bandwidth is very large, practical wideband systems are prone to spatial wideband effects/beam squint (Han and Danijela, 2019; Chen *et al.*, 2021*a*). Apart from the frequency-selective nature, the frequency domain channel at each carrier will be a function of AoAs and AoDs in this case. Extending the above design for cell discovery considering beam squint can be interesting and will be considered in the future.

4.6   COMPARISON OF MUTUAL COHERENCE VALUES

We compare the mutual coherence of the proposed MUBB training scheme with the random beamforming scheme (RBF) (Han and Danijela, 2019; Alkhateeb *et al.*, 2015; Manoj and Kannu, 2018; Wang *et al.*, 2016) in Table 4.1. For the RBF scheme the entries in the beamforming matrices are randomly chosen from QPSK symbols $\pm 1 \pm j$ (and suitably normalized to unit column norm). The coherence properties of the RBF scheme are analyzed in (Manoj and Kannu, 2018). The mutual coherence of $\bar{\bar{\Psi}}$ for RBF and MUBB schemes with $N_t = 32 \times 8$ and $N_r = 4 \times 2$ is given in Table 4.1.

We note that the reduction factors u_1 and u_2 in our design affect the number of transmit beamforming weights Q, the training phase duration $M = \frac{PQ}{N_{\mathrm{rf}}}$, the number of unique transmit beamforming matrices $I_{\max}$ and the mutual coherence μ of the resulting sensing matrix. The mutual coherence is computed assuming $N_B \leq I_{\max}$, in which case, the μ solely depends on the beamforming weights and not on the synchronization signal transmitted (Please refer to Theorem 7). This can be considered as the case of $N_S = 1$, with no separate synchronization signal being transmitted. For the non-separable scheme, we set the reduction factor u as the sum of the reduction factors along azimuth u_1 and elevation u_2 directions. For the MUBB scheme with coarse/wider beams, we set the beam combining factors along azimuth and elevation directions in (3.20) as $\alpha_1 = 2^{u_1}$ and $\alpha_2 = 2^{u_2}$, respectively.

For the RBF scheme, we generate the same number of unique beamforming matrices as the MUBB scheme, which is given by $I_{\max}$. In fact, we generate hundreds of sets, with each set containing $I_{\max}$ random beamforming matrices and pick the set which gives the smallest coherence. RBF scheme requires these random matrices to be stored at the transmitter and receiver, which necessitates large storage at UE and BSs, especially when antenna dimensions are large.

From Table 4.1, we note that the mutual coherence value for MUBB scheme is considerably small when compared with the RBF scheme for all the cases. We would like to direct the attention to the last row of Table 4.1, which indicates that, using suitable design parameters (u_1, u_2), we can generate 128 unique transmit beamforming matrices with low coherence, which enables cell discovery in a network with as many BSs, using a training phase of duration $M = 256$ (without transmitting any BS specific SS). We will study this scenario further in the following section using simulation results.

Table 4.1: Mutual coherence of $\bar{\mathbf{\Psi}}$ for different training schemes: $N_t = 32 \times 16$, $N_r = 4 \times 2$, $N_S = 1$, $N_{\text{rf}} = 4$. Legends 's' and 'ns' denotes separable and non-separable schemes respectively.

Scheme	(u_1, u_2)	$\frac{PQ}{N_{\text{rf}}}$	$I_{\max}$	Mutual Coherence μ			
				MUBB-s	RBF-s	MUBB-ns	RBF - ns
Without widen.	$(2, 1)$	64	4	0.5	0.7603	0.1768	0.4169
	$(1, 1)$	128	16	0.5	0.6644	0.125	0.3563
	$(1, 0)$	256	64	0.3536	0.4906	0.0884	.2606
	(u_1, u_2)	$\frac{PQ}{N_{\text{rf}}}$	I_{max}	MUBB$^{(w)}$-s	RBF$^{(w)}$-s	MUBB$^{(w)}$-ns	RBF$^{(w)}$-ns
With widen.	$(3, 2)$	16	8	0.7071	0.7289	0.3536	0.5660
	$(2, 1)$	64	32	0.5	0.5345	0.1768	0.4110
	$(1, 0)$	256	128	0.3536	0.4859	0.0884	0.2600

4.7 COMPLEXITY ANALYSIS

The overhead involved can be divided into three parts: training overhead, algorithm complexity and storage complexity.

4.7.1 Training Overhead and Algorithm Complexity

Training overhead is characterized by the number of pilot transmission and is analyzed in detail in the simulation section. The computational complexity of the algorithm is based on the number of complex multiplications and additions needed to implement the detection rule for each algorithm. The detection rule for CBS is specified in (3.26) and (3.27) in the thesis. The computation for the test statistic $z_{p,q,i}$ for a fixed (p, q, i) in eq (3.26) requires N_S complex multiplications and $N_S - 1$ complex additions. Energy calculation in (3.27) requires 1 complex multiplication. Thus the total complexity can be obtained as in Table 4.2 by considering all the beam combinations and BS identities. The same detection rule holds true for BC scenario as well. However, with a recombination matrix defined as in (3.16), the wider beams will be indexed as $p = 1, ..., \frac{N_r}{\beta}, q = 1, ..., \frac{N_t}{\alpha}$. The complexity for BC is given in Table 4.2. Note that the CBS method uses finer beams and the BC scheme uses wider beams and cannot be implemented vice-versa.

For MUB and RBF methods, the detection rule is given in (4.3). As discussed in Section 4.2, with the reduction parameters set as (u_1, u_2), the total number of received symbols is given by MN_S, where $M = \frac{N_t N_r}{2^u}$ and $u = u_1 + u_2$. For M received symbols at the UE, for any column index l, the computation of $|[\bar{\Psi}]^*_{:,l}\bar{y}|^2$ requires $MN_S + 1$ complex multiplications and $MN_S - 1$ complex additions. However, further reduction in complexity can be achieved for MUBB scheme by exploiting the structure. For simplicity, we will explain the same by considering $l = 1$. Hence

$$z_1 = [\bar{\Psi}]^*_{:,1}\bar{y} = \left(\mathbf{x}^{(1)} \otimes [\Psi^{(1)}]_{:,1}\right)^* \bar{y} = \left(\mathbf{x}^{(1)*} \otimes [\Psi^{(1)}]^*_{:,1}\right)\bar{y} \qquad (4.23)$$

Here $(.)^*$ is the Hermitian operator and hence $\mathbf{x}^{(1)*} \otimes [\Psi^{(1)}]^*_{:,1}$ will be a row vector. As defined in (4.1) and (4.2), $\mathbf{y} = [\mathbf{y}_1^T, \mathbf{y}_2^T, ..., \mathbf{y}_{N_S}^T]$ and $\mathbf{x}^{(1)} = [x_1^{(1)} x_2^{(1)}, ..., x_{N_S}^{(1)}]$. Then, above equation can be written as

$$z_1 = \left[x_1^{(1)*}[\Psi^{(1)}]^*_{:,1}, \cdots, x_{N_S}^{(1)*}[\Psi^{(1)}]^*_{:,1}\right] \begin{bmatrix} \mathbf{y}_1 \\ \mathbf{y}_2 \\ \vdots \\ \mathbf{y}_{N_S} \end{bmatrix}$$

$$= x_1^{(1)*}[\Psi^{(1)}]^*_{:,1}\mathbf{y}_1 + \cdots + x_{N_S}^{(1)*}[\Psi^{(1)}]^*_{:,1}\mathbf{y}_{N_S} \qquad (4.24)$$

Now, for MUBB, the entries of the $\Psi^{(1)}$ matrix consists of scaled entries from the set

$+1, -1, +j, -j$. Thus each of the terms $[\mathbf{\Psi}^{(1)}]^{*}_{:,1}\mathbf{y}_1, ..., [\mathbf{\Psi}^{(1)}]^{*}_{:,1}\mathbf{y}_{N_S}$ can be computed without any complex multiplication but by arranging the real and imaginary parts and $M - 1$ complex additions. Thus eq (4.23) can be implemented with N_S complex multiplications and $MN_S - 1$ complex additions.

QPSK symbols are the entries of $\Psi^{(1)}$ matrix for RBF method. Hence, the computation of the products, $[\mathbf{\Psi}^{(1)}]^{*}_{:,1}\mathbf{y}_1, ..., [\mathbf{\Psi}^{(1)}]^{*}_{:,1}\mathbf{y}_{N_S}$ can be done with complex additions alone. Particularly, each term involves 1 additions corresponding to 1 of the product terms and thus a total of $2M - 1$ complex additions. Thus, $2MN_S - 1$ complex additions and N_S complex multiplications are required to implement (4.23) for RBF.

The total complexity can be then computed by taking into account the complexity of finding the energy of z_1. It can be seen that the above complexity calculations holds true for all the column index l and the total complexity can be calculated by considering all the columns of $\bar{\mathbf{\Psi}}$. The number of columns of $\bar{\mathbf{\Psi}}$ is $N_t N_r N_B$ for MUBB and RBF schemes. MUBB^{w} and RBF^{w} methods use coarser beams and thus the model in (4.15) yields the total number of $\frac{N_t N_r N_B}{\alpha\beta}$ columns in the resulting $\bar{\mathbf{\Psi}}$ matrix. Here α and β are the combining/grouping factors that allows flexibility of grouping of channel matrix entries, thereby permitting training using lesser number of widened beams. The results are summarised in Table 4.2 and the training durations are mentioned in Table 4.3. All the schemes require same number of complex multiplications. MUBB requires a higher number of complex additions compared to that of CBS and BC schemes, however the complexity is still lesser than the RBF method. Also, when compared with generalised compressive sensing methods with arbitrary entries in the Ψ matrix, MUBB method allows for a large saving in the number of complex multiplications and additions. The training duration for different methods are given in 4.3.

Table 4.2: Computation complexity of different CD schemes

Complexity	CBS	BC	MUBB	RBF
Training using Finer Beams, $L = N_t N_r N_B$				
# Multiplications	$L(N_S+1)$	–	$L(N_S+1)$	$L(N_S+1)$
# Additions	$L(N_S-1)$	–	$L(MN_S-1)$	$L(2MN_S-1)$
Training using widened beams, $L = \frac{N_t N_r}{\alpha\beta} N_B$				
# Multiplications	–	$L(N_S+1)$	$L(N_S+1)$	$L(N_S+1)$
# Additions	–	$L(N_S-1)$	$L(MN_S-1)$	$L(2MN_S-1)$

Table 4.3: Training duration M of different CD schemes. α, β : Beam combining factors, u : Training reduction parameter.

Training beams	CBS	BC	MUBB	RBF
Fine	$N_t N_r$	–	$\frac{N_t N_r}{2^u}$	$\frac{N_t N_r}{2^u}$
Coarse	–	$\frac{N_t N_r}{\alpha\beta}$	$\frac{N_t N_r}{2^u \alpha\beta}$	$\frac{N_t N_r}{2^u \alpha\beta}$

4.7.2 Storage Complexity

The receiver algorithm for CBS and BC methods discussed in (3.26) and (3.27) requires the SS of all the N_B BSs in the network stored at the UE. This incurs for a total of $N_S \times N_B$ complex data. Additionally, as given in (4.2) and (4.3), the $\boldsymbol{\Psi}$ matrix also needs to be stored at the UE for MUBB and RBF algorithms, contributing to an additional storage requisite of $M \times \frac{N_t N_r}{\alpha\beta} N_B$ complex matrix at the UE.

4.8 SIMULATION RESULTS

In this section, we present simulation results comparing the cell detection performance of various beamforming training schemes with a constraint on the probability of false alarm. Particularly, we compare MUBB, RBF, and BC schemes. Note that the BC scheme is similar to the CD scheme standardized by 3GPP as a part of NR specification (Giordani *et al.*, 2019*a*). The network set up and the mmWave channel generation is done as explained in Section 3.5.1.

4.8.1 Detection Performance with Widened Beams

We set $N_B = 100$, $N_A = 4$ and the synchronization signals as SSS sequences from 5G-NR ($N_S = 128$). For the low resolution model (4.15), Figure 4.2 shows the detection performance of MUBB$^{(w)}$, BC and RBF$^{(w)}$ schemes, as a function of the parameter $M = \frac{PQ}{N_{rf}}$, which governs the training duration. We observe that the $\mathbb{P}_D$ value for cell discovery schemes with non-separable antenna configuration outperforms that of the separable antenna configuration. Note that the mutual coherence of the sensing matrix will be smaller for non-separable configuration when compared to that of the separable configuration. We also see that our proposed MUBB$^{(w)}$ scheme outperforms the corresponding RBF$^{(w)}$ and BC schemes in terms of detection performance for both separable and non-separable antenna configurations. MUBB$^{(w)}$ non-separable configuration with $M = 16$ attains almost similar performance as that of the BC scheme with $M = 64$.

4.8.2 Comparison of Detection using Wider and Finer Beams

We compare the performance of detection using wider beams (based on low-resolution beamspace matrix (4.15)) and finer beams (based on full resolution beamspace matrix (3.5)) in Figure 4.3. With finer beams (indicated by legends MUBB and RBF), the

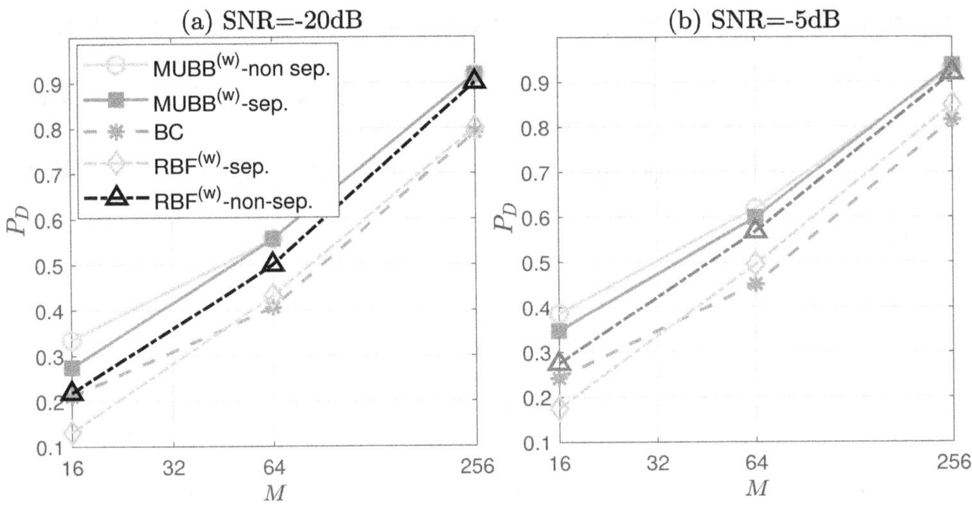

Figure 4.2: Detection Performance using SSS sequences ($N_S = 128$).

minimum value of the training duration parameter M required for successful detection is 32 for non-separable configuration (64 for separable configuration). For the separable configuration, detection using wider beams perform well for small M values, while finer beams work well for larger M. For non-separable configuration, the training scheme using finer beams outperforms the training scheme with wider beams for all M values (above the minimum requirement). Our results reveal that, when the training phase is small, it is better to search using wider beams. On the other hand, we can use finer beams when the training duration is large.

4.8.3 Average Beamforming SNR of the detected BS

Based on the largest detector metric $|z_l|^2$ (with $z_l = [\bar{\mathbf{\Psi}}]^*_{:,l}\bar{\mathbf{y}}$), we get the identity of the detected BS i_0 and the corresponding AoA-AoD location (p_0, q_0) in the beamspace matrix. The data transfer phase can employ the DFT-based beams based on the

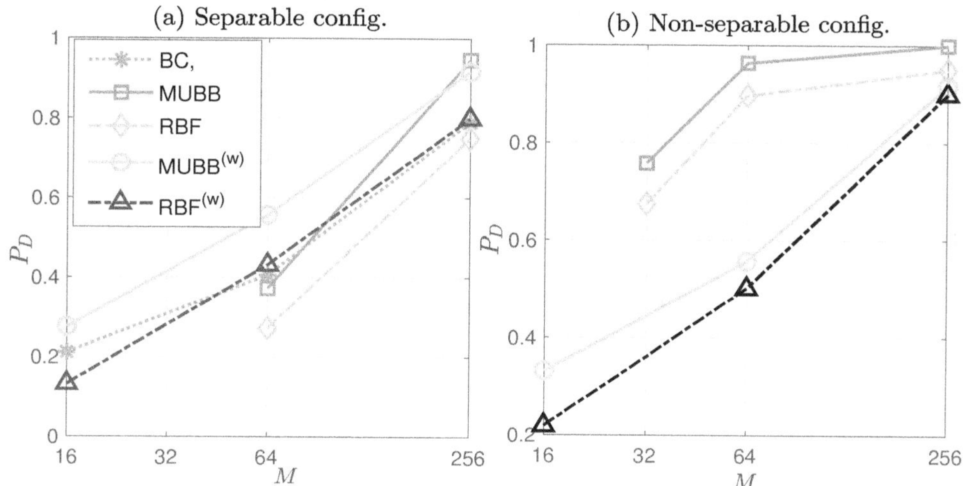

Figure 4.3: Detection Performance with finer and wider beams at SNR = -20dB.

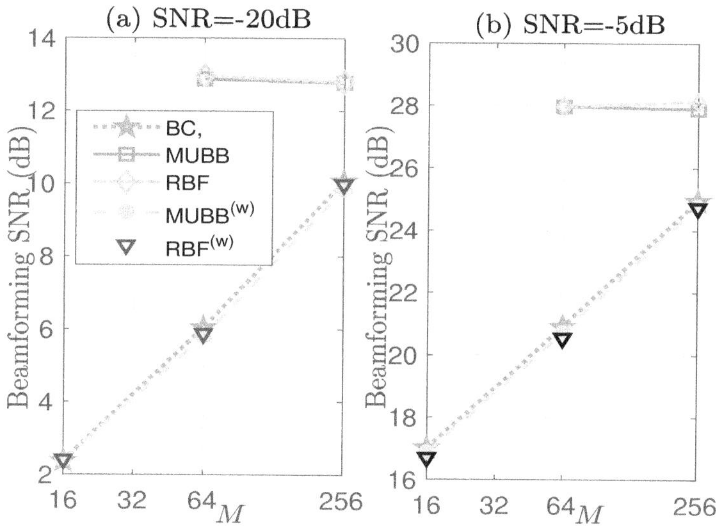

Figure 4.4: Comparison of Beamforming SNR with separable antenna configuration.

identified AoA-AoD pair to achieve the beamforming gain with the detected BS. Now, we study the *average beamforming SNR* achieved by the various training schemes. Specifically, with $\mathbf{w}_t = [\bar{\mathbf{F}}_{N_t}]_{:,q_0}$ and $\mathbf{w}_r = [\bar{\mathbf{F}}_{N_r}]_{:,p_0}$ being the beamforming directions, we define the beamforming SNR as, $\dfrac{\left| \sqrt{\rho_{i_0}} \, \mathbf{w}_r^H \mathbf{H}_{i_0} \mathbf{w}_t \right|^2}{\sigma_n^2}$.

We average this beamforming SNR over multiple channel realizations under the condition that the detected BS is an active BS. The simulation results are shown in

Figure 4.4 for separable antenna configuration. With the increase in the value of M, the resolution of the beamspace search (4.15) gets finer and results in a steady increase in the beamforming SNR with M for MUBB$^{(w)}$, BC and RBF$^{(w)}$ methods. Further, the average beamforming SNR performance for these coarse beamforming schemes are very much comparable for different M values as the angle resolution/beam width is the same for all these schemes for a fixed M. Secondly, for training schemes without beam combining, the algorithm senses the beamspace matrix at its full resolution (3.5) irrespective of M, as explained in Section 4.2. Hence, the average beamforming SNR of MUBB and RBF schemes remains unchanged with M. Also, the full-resolution search gives better beamforming SNR when compared to the search using coarser/wider beams, which justifies our explanation (Section 3.3.2) on the reduction in beamforming gain due to combining the uncorrelated entries of the beamspace matrix. Note that the angular resolution and hence the beamforming SNR performance for a fixed M remains the same when non-separable antenna configuration is used instead of separable set-up.

4.8.4 Successful Detection using MUB sequences

In order to validate the use of sequences other than SSS sequences, we quantify the successful detection of at least one active BS when MUB sequences are transmitted by the BSs in Figure 4.5(a) and (b). We evaluate the performance when the number of BSs present in the network is $N_B = 1000$. With $N_S = 32$, we can get 1024 MUB sequences (using MUB matrices for dimension 32) and assign any 1000 of them to each BS. As shown in Figure 4.5(a), $\mathbb{P}_D$ plots show the same trend as in Figure 4.2. The reasoning and findings in Section 4.8.1 holds true in this case as the number of active BSs and the

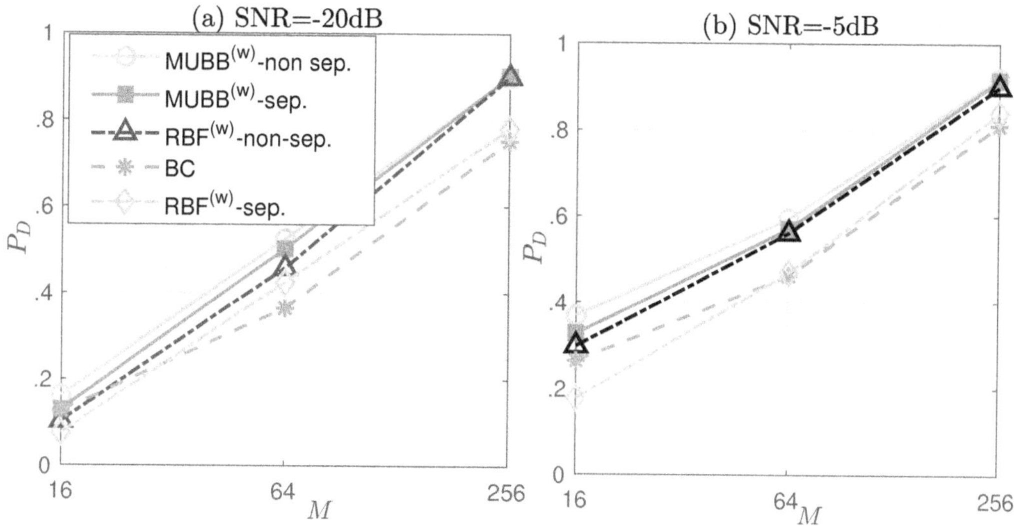

Figure 4.5: Detection Performance with MUB sequence transmission ($N_S = 32$).

beamforming matrices are the same for both scenarios. When compared to Figure 4.2 (for which $N_S = 128$), we see a decrease in the discovery performance when SNR becomes -20 dB in Figure 4.5(a). This shows that the detection performance at lower SNRs can be improved by using larger-length synchronization signals, at the expense of the additional training overhead.

4.8.5 Cell discovery without Sequence Transmission

If the total number of BSs N_B is less than $I_{\max}$ from the MUBB design, we can assign unique beamforming matrices for each BS, which can accomplish cell discovery at the UE without transmitting any BS-specific synchronization signal (that is, we can set $N_S = 1$). As given in the last row of Table 4.1, an mmWave network with 128 BSs can be supported by MUBB scheme by using coarser training beams and setting the reduction factors u_1, u_2 as mentioned in Table 4.1.

Table 4.4: Mutual coherence of $\bar{\boldsymbol{\Psi}}$ for different training schemes in Figure 4.6

Scheme	N_S	Training Duration (MN_S)	Beam-width (α_1, α_2)	μ
MUBB$^{(w)}$-sep	1	256	(2,1)	0.3536
RBF$^{(w)}$-sep	1	256	(2,1)	0.5049
MUBB$^{(w)}$-non sep	1	256	(2,1)	0.0884
RBF$^{(w)}$-non sep	1	256	(2,1)	0.2661
BC	16	4096	(2,1)	0.25
BC	16	256	(8,4)	0.25

To study this scenario, we set $N_B = 128, N_A = 4, N_S = 1$ and study the detection performance with the training duration of $MN_S = 256$. As the BC scheme uses the same training beamforming vectors for all the BSs, the UE cannot identify the active base station unless a synchronization signal specific to each BS is transmitted. For comparison, we consider two different BC schemes which transmit BS-specific MUB sequences of length $N_S = 16$. One BC scheme keeps the same training phase duration ($MN_S = 256$) by increasing the beam combining factors α_1 and α_2 for BC scheme (3.20) appropriately (that is, search using wider beams). The other BC scheme uses the same beam widths as the MUBB scheme, but the training duration increases to $MN_s = 4096$.

The μ values for different schemes under consideration are summarised in 4.4. All the BSs use the same set of DFT-based training beams in BC scheme. Hence the mutual coherence for BC method depends only on the maximum correlation between different transmit sequences, ζ. For BC method with MUB based sequences, when $N_B > 1$,

$$\mu = \zeta = \frac{1}{\sqrt{N_S}}.$$

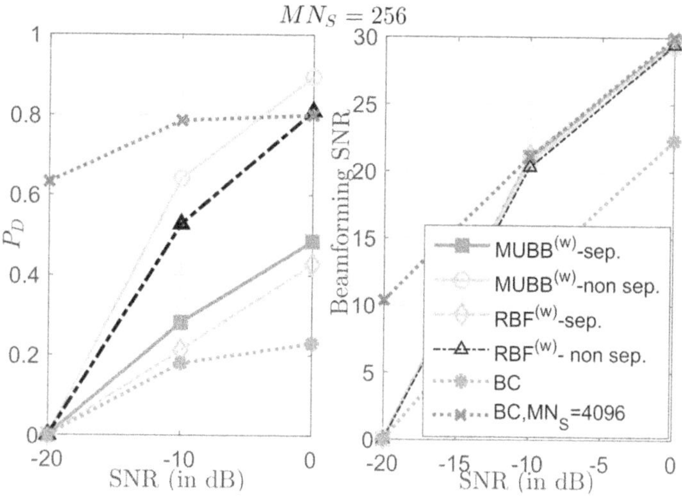

Figure 4.6: Detection without synchronization signal transmission ($N_S = 1$).

The results in Figure 4.6 show that, among the schemes with the same training duration, MUBB$^{(w)}$ performs the best, and the beamforming SNR gain is almost 8 dB higher than the corresponding BC scheme. BC scheme with much larger training duration $MN_S = 4096$ performs well at low SNR (at the expense of excessive training overhead) but still performs poorer than the proposed MUBB$^{(w)}$ non-separable scheme when SNR is close to 0 dB. BC schemes with very wide beams $(\alpha_1, \alpha_2) = (8, 4)$ performs poorly due to the reduction in the beamforming gain, as discussed in Section 3.3.2.

4.8.6   Analysis for Wideband channel model

In this section, we analyze the cell discovery performance for wideband mmWave systems discussed in Section 4.5 by considering a UPA set up with $N_A = 4$ and $N_B = 16$. The number of channel taps in the discrete domain is set as $N_c = 4$ and hence $N_{cp} > N_c$ is fixed as 8. The bandwidth is selected as $57.6MHz$ as specified in the 5G NR framework, and the channel path delays are taken as uniformly distributed

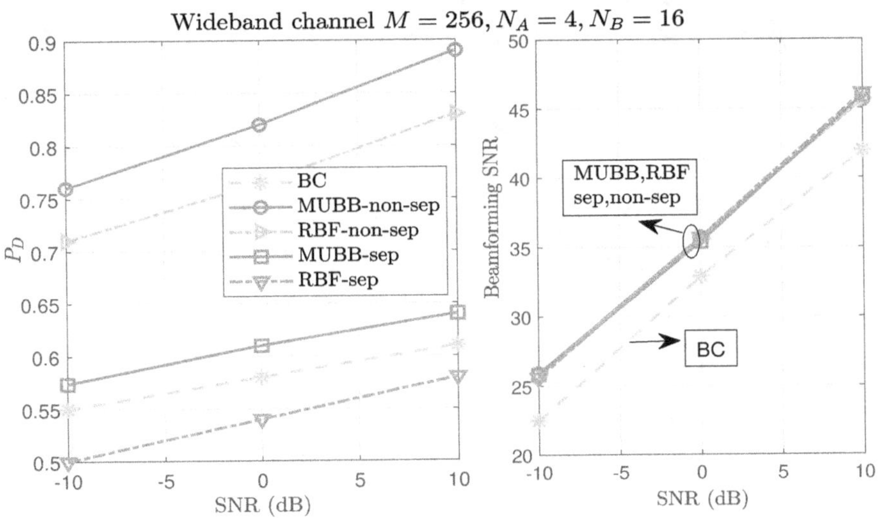

Figure 4.7: Detection with wideband channel model

in the interval $[0$ to $N_c(T_s - 1)]$ where T_s is the sampling rate and is equal to the inverse

of the bandwidth. Channels are generated based on the Saleh-Valenzuela model given

in (4.19)

In Figure 4.7, we plot the probability of detecting one BS, $\mathbb{P}_D$, versus SNR when

M is fixed as 256 and finer beams are used for training. We observe the superior

performance of the MUBB scheme over RBF and BC methods for all the SNR values.

BC outperforms the RBF separable scheme in terms of detection. However, the

attained beamforming SNR is low because of the reduced beam resolution. Our results

demonstrate the applicability of the MUB-based training schemes in the wideband

systems as well.

4.8.7 Detection performance with GBOMP algorithm

MUB-based training schemes developed in this work provide a deterministic way of

constructing the sensing matrices with small mutual coherence for the compressive

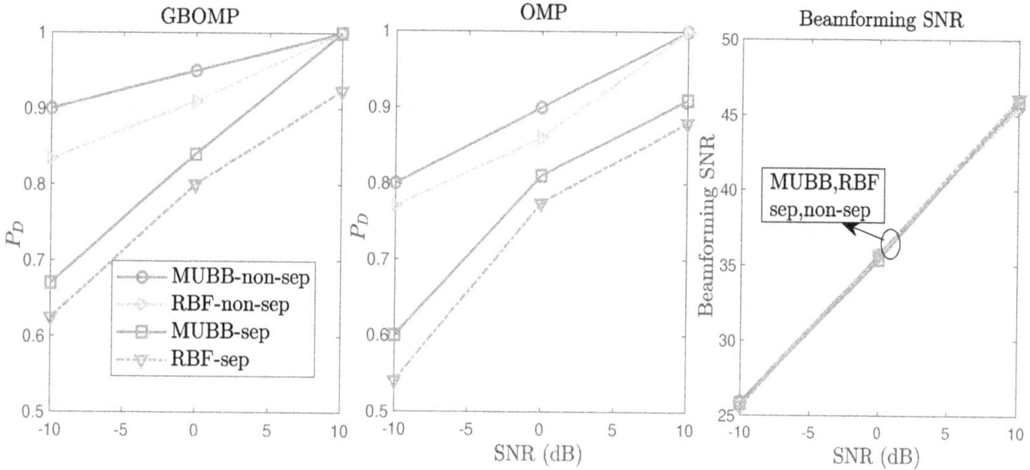

Figure 4.8: Detection with OMP and GBOMP based algorithms ($N_S = 1, MN_S = 256$). The beamforming SNR performance is the same for both algorithms, as shown in the rightmost figure.

sensing formulation for cell discovery. Such a training method can be used in conjunction with any UE algorithm whose detection depends on the mutual coherence of the sensing matrix. As noted earlier, the FFT bins closer to the spatial frequencies of the true AoA-AoD pairs will have significant entries in the beamspace channel matrix $\mathbf{G}_i$, due to the spectral leakage. Hence, the beamspace channel matrix exhibits block sparse structure. Exploiting this block sparse strcture, a generalized block OMP (GBOMP) algorithm is given in (Manoj and Kannu, 2018), for estimating the entries of the beamspace channel matrices. In this section, we use a single run of GBOMP algorithm to identify the signficant entries of the beamspace channel matrices and compare the performance with the stagewise OMP algorithm in Figure 4.8.

We fix the number of BSs as $N_A = 4$ and $N_B = 64$. M is set as 256 and $N_S = 1$. We notice that the GBOMP algorithm shows better detection performance compared with

OMP, especially at low SNRs, since GBOMP method exploits the block sparse nature of the channel matrix. We also plot the beamforming SNR as defined in Section 4.8.3 in Figure 4.8. As discussed in Section 4.8.3, beamforming SNR depends mainly on the beam width/resolution. In other words, the beamforming SNR varries for finer and widened beam based CD schemes. Here, we compare both OMP and GBOMP algorithms with the finer beams of same resolution, thus their beamforming SNR gains are similar. We also observe that the MUB-based training scheme outperforms the RBF scheme for both separable and non-separable configurations.

4.8.8   Peformance with ULA configuration

In Figure 4.9, we plot $\mathbb{P}_D$ and beamforming gain of different training schemes using ULA. We fix $N_A = 4$ and $N_B = 16$. For CBS and BC schemes, MUB sequences of length $N_S = 4$ are used to support 16 BSs, while we implement MUBB and RBF schemes without sequence transmission (ie $N_S = 1$). The performance for ULA case is similar to that of UPA case as observed in Figure 4.6. Further, we see the better performance of MUBB and RBF schemes over their respective widened versions with respect to both $\mathbb{P}_D$ and γ. The MUBB$^{(w)}$ and RBF$^{(w)}$ schemes are preferred when the number of BSs is very large, and cell discovery needs to be accomplished with lesser number of measurements, and the scheme aims at detecting BSs at the expense of beamforming gain.

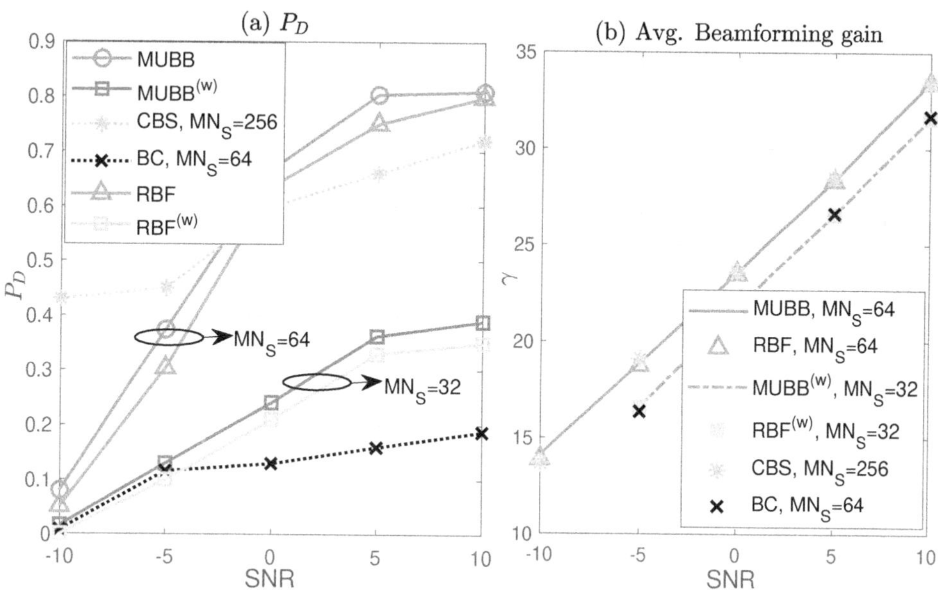

Figure 4.9: Probability of detecting at least one BS using ULA configuration. For CBS and BC, MUB transmit sequences of length 4 are used. MUBB and RBF schemes are implemented without sequence transmission

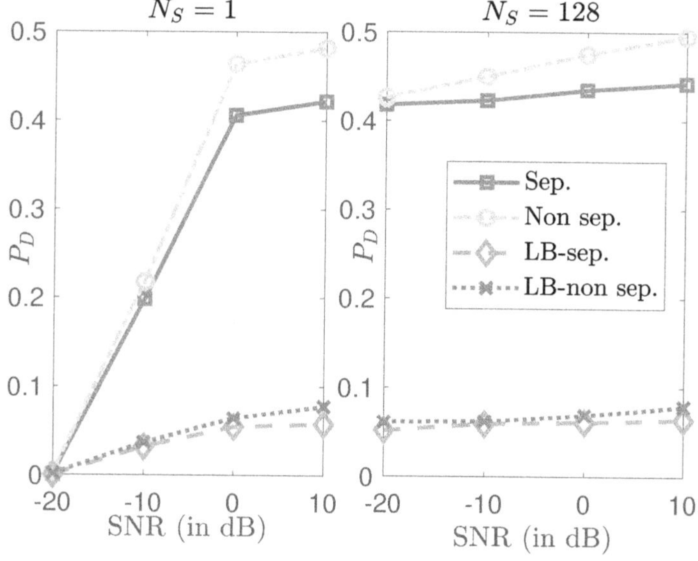

Figure 4.10: Comparison of the Lower bound for $\mathbb{P}_D$ with MUBB scheme. $N_B = 2$ and No. of paths per BS=1

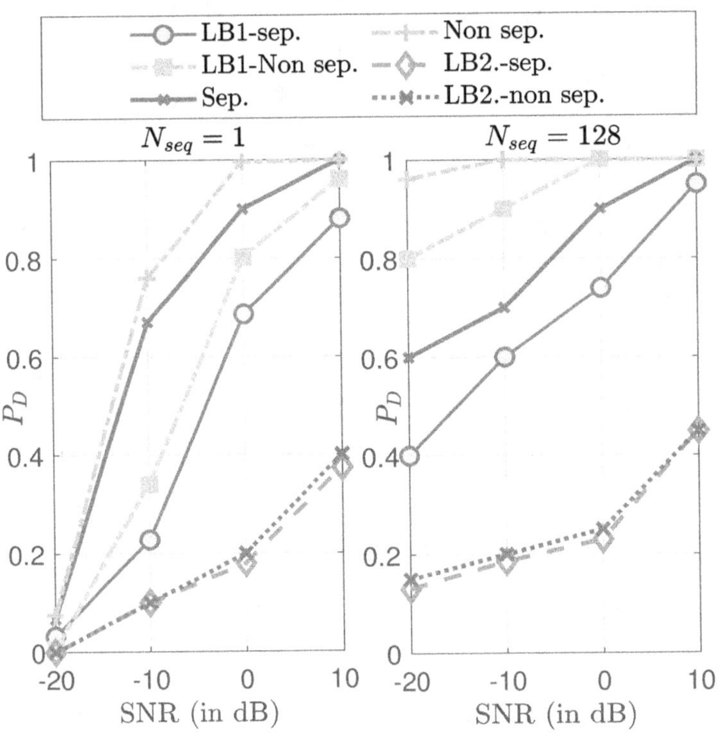

Figure 4.11: Comparison of the analytical $\mathbb{P}_D$ expressions of MUBB method for on-grid channels. $N_B = 2$ and No. of paths, $K = [1, 1]$

4.8.9 Comparing Analytical $\mathbb{P}_D$ values with Simulation Results

We compare the analytical detection probability bound from Theorem 6 with the numerical results. Towards that, we generate the channels as per the expressions in (2.3) with $N_A = 2$ without search space restriction and generate the observations as in (3.2). For simplicity, BSs are assumed to have only single path. We fix the MUBB reduction parameter $(u_1, u_2) = (2, 1)$ which results in $M = 128$ with $N_{\text{rf}} = 4$. The $\mathbb{P}_D$ values from simulations and analytical lower bounds (denoted by legends LB) are shown in Figure 4.10 for $N_S = 1$ and 128. The analytical bounds are loose, but they reveal the connections to the mutual coherence parameter and reflect the detection trend from simulation results.

For the special case when the multipath AoAs and AoDs coincide with the quantized angles of the sparsifying DFT grid, the channel matrix $\mathbf{G}_i$ becomes exactly sparse. We term this idealized channel as *on-grid channel*. For the on-grid channels, the insignificant entries g_b in the beamspace matrices (4.4) become identical to 0. We consider two active BSs and each BS has a single path. We compute the lower bound for the $\mathbb{P}_D$ expression given in (4.6) (denoted by legend "LB-1") using all the eigenvalues of $\mathbf{R}_{z_a}$ and the lower bound based on the smallest eigenvalue as given in (4.7) (denoted by legend "LB-2"). Since LB-1 uses all the eigenvalues of $\mathbf{R}_{z_a}$, LB-1 is a tighter bound when compared with LB-2. The results in Figure 4.11 show the the analytical $\mathbb{P}_D$ bounds matches well with the simulation curves, for the on-grid channels.

4.9   SUMMARY

In this chapter, we formulated the cell discovery problem as a sparse signal recovery problem and developed training beamforming vectors using Mutually Unbiased Bases (MUBB), which resulted in sensing matrices with low mutual coherence. We included parameters for the same to control the training phase duration without affecting the beamforming gain. For the MUB design, we analytically characterized the relationship between training phase duration and the corresponding mutual coherence values. In order to achieve fast cell discovery, we also provided ways to reduce the training phase duration by using wider/combined beams and incorporated them with the MUBB. We also explained on how our proposed schemes can be incorporated with the 5G-NR framework for cell discovery, wideband systems, and other sparse recovery-based UE algorithms. Our simulation studies with NYUSIM mmWave channels established that

MUBB performs better than the conventional beam sweeping and random beamforming schemes in terms of detection probability and post-beamforming SNR. We showed the relevance of using a coarser beam search for smaller training duration and a finer beam search for better directivity. With suitable design parameters in the MUBB scheme, we generated more than a hundred unique transmit beamforming matrices and showed that cell discovery could be accomplished in a network with more than a hundred BS, without transmitting any BS-specific synchronization signal.

CHAPTER 5

Channel estimation using MUB based training vectors

The key enabling technologies adapted in 5G, like massive MIMO architecture, millimeter wave communication, dense small cells, etc., help realize the high data rate demands in 5G at low latency. 5G also supports a massive number of simultaneous users and relies heavily on multi-user and multi-beam transmissions with good interference management. However, these requirements can be achieved only by using appropriate precoding, which in turn relies on accurate cell discovery and wireless channel estimation. Cell discovery involves the process of finding at least one accessible directional path to a base station. Channel estimation is a more complex problem in which the user estimates the entire channel itself. Similar to the cell discovery problem, channel estimation is challenging in massive MIMO mmWave systems due to the fast-changing channel and the large channel matrix dimensions. Compressive sensing-based approaches for mmWave channel estimation have garnished a lot of importance and are shown to have significant improvement over traditional methods as they become extremely complicated when applied to systems with large antenna dimensions. In this chapter, we formulate the channel estimation as a sparse vector recovery problem and use the MUB-based beamforming vectors constructed in Chapter 4 for the training portion for narrowband channel estimation. We consider hybrid beamforming architecture with multiple BSs in the network. The proposed training scheme can be applied generally to any sparse signal recovery problem and user algorithms relying on the lower mutual coherent sensing matrix can be applied. We study the performance with two different receiver algorithms, Orthogonal Matching

Pursuit (OMP) and Generalised Block Orthogonal Matching Pursuit (BGOMP), and compare the results using MUBB, RBF, and beam sweeping schemes.

5.1   CHANNEL ESTIMATION PROBLEM

The system model remains the same for cell discovery and channel estimation problems. Recall the sparse signal model in (4.2),

$$\bar{\mathbf{y}} = \bar{\boldsymbol{\Psi}}\mathbf{g} + \bar{\mathbf{n}}. \tag{5.1}$$

Here $\bar{\mathbf{y}}$ is the received signal vector, and $\bar{\mathbf{n}}$ is the associated additive Complex Gaussian noise. $\mathbf{g}$ is the appended mmWave channel vector, and $\bar{\boldsymbol{\Psi}}$ is the sensing matrix consisting of the transmit pilot signals and the beamforming vectors. In the cell discovery problem, the focus was on detecting at least one significant entry in $\mathbf{g}$. However, the entire $\mathbf{g}$ vector needs to be estimated for channel estimation.

5.2   SPARSE MODEL AND RECEIVER ALGORITHM

We have explained the sparse nature of the mmWave channels in Section 2.4 of Chapter 2. The signal model in (5.1) is according to the general sparse vector recovery problem, and any sparse signal recovery algorithm can be used to recover/estimate the entries of $\mathbf{g}$. This thesis focuses on the construction of an appropriate sensing matrix using the MUB-based beamforming vectors for the training phase and hence can be incorporated with any receiver algorithm that depends on the lower mutual coherence of the sensing matrix. Many algorithms have been proposed in the literature for sparse signal recovery, however, in this work, we use the classic Orthogonal Matching Pursuit (OMP) algorithm and a modified version called Generalised Block OMP (GBOMP) (Manoj and Kannu, 2018) algorithm for channel estimation. GBOMP is specifically applicable for mmWave channels. We will discuss these algorithms briefly in the next section.

Using the estimate of $\mathbf{g}$ (we refer to the estimate as $\hat{\mathbf{g}}$) obtained using OMP or GBOMP algorithm, the beamspace channel vectors for individual BSs can be obtained by appropriate partitioning. The beamspace matrices $\mathbf{G}_i$ can be obtained by the reverse transformation of the vectorization process, which gives the channel matrices $\mathbf{H}_i$ by inverse DFT transformation. For schemes using widened beams, the OMP/GBOMP algorithm can only estimate the effective lower resolution channel matrix of any BS, $\mathbf{G}^{(w)}$, given in (3.18). By vectorizing the matrix, the transformation can be written as

$$\mathbf{g}_i^{(w)} = \mathrm{vec}(\mathbf{G}_i^{(w)}) = \underbrace{\left[\mathbf{S}_{N_t,\alpha}^{*} \otimes \mathbf{S}_{N_r,\beta}^{*}\right]}_{\mathbf{S}} \mathbf{g}_i. \tag{5.2}$$

Now suppose $\hat{\mathbf{g}}_i^{(w)}$ is the estimate obtained using the receiver algorithm. The full resolution channel estimate, $\hat{\mathbf{g}}_i$, can be obtained by the left inverse transformation operation of the above equation. That is,

$$\hat{\mathbf{g}}_i = \mathbf{S}^{*}(\mathbf{S}\mathbf{S}^{*})^{-1}\hat{\mathbf{g}}_i^{(w)} = \mathbf{S}^{*}\hat{\mathbf{g}}_i^{(w)} \tag{5.3}$$

Here we use the property that $\mathbf{S}\mathbf{S}^{*} = \mathbf{I}$. Note that transformation from $\mathbf{g}_i$ to $\mathbf{g}_i^{(w)}$ combines the entries and is not invertible. The reverse transformation in (5.3) is hence the best approximation of $\mathbf{g}_i$ possible.

5.2.1 OMP algorithm

OMP is a greedy iterative sparse recovery algorithm widely used for mmWave channel estimation (Lee *et al.*, 2016*b*; Manoj and Kannu, 2018), in which one column of the sensing matrix is picked in each iteration that results in the best estimate of the vector to be estimated. The vector recovery performance majorly depends on the mutual coherence of the sensing matrix. The procedure for the implementation of the OMP algorithm for estimation of $\mathbf{g}$ in (5.1) is given in **Algorithm 1**.

Algorithm 1 :OMP

---

  1. Input $\bar{\mathbf{y}}$ and $\bar{\boldsymbol{\Psi}}$

  2. Initialize: $\mathbf{r}_1 \leftarrow \bar{\mathbf{y}}, \mathbf{r}_0 = \mathbf{0}, \mathcal{I} = \phi$, iteration variable,i $=1$

while $i \leq i_{\max}$ or $||r_i - r_{i-1}||^2 < \tau^{\mathrm{OMP}}$ **do**

    3. Find $l_i = \underset{l}{\mathrm{argmax}}|\bar{\boldsymbol{\Psi}}_l^H \mathbf{r}_i|^2$

    4. Update index set, $\mathcal{I} \leftarrow \mathcal{I} \cup l_i$

    5. Find the least squares solution for the weight vector, $\mathbf{x}_i = \left(\bar{\boldsymbol{\Psi}}_{\mathcal{I}}^H \bar{\boldsymbol{\Psi}}_{\mathcal{I}}\right)^{-1} \bar{\boldsymbol{\Psi}}_{\mathcal{I}}^H \bar{\mathbf{y}}$

    Note: $\mathbf{x}_i$ specifies the entries of $\hat{\mathbf{g}}_{\mathcal{I}}$ in the ith iteration.

    6. $i \leftarrow i+1$

    7. Update residue, $r_i \leftarrow \bar{\mathbf{y}} - \bar{\boldsymbol{\Psi}}_{\mathcal{I}} \mathbf{x}_{i-1}$

end while

  7. Estimate, $\hat{\mathbf{g}}_{\mathcal{I}} = \mathbf{x}_{i-1}; \hat{\mathbf{g}}_{\mathcal{I}^c} = \mathbf{0}$

The inputs to the OMP algorithm are $\bar{\mathbf{y}}$ and $\bar{\boldsymbol{\Psi}}$. OMP works on updating the residue vector $\mathbf{r}_i$ in each iteration by finding and eliminating the contribution of the best correlating column of the sensing matrix and calculating the closest approximation of the g vector based on the identified column. In Step 2 of **Algorithm 1**, residue is initialized as $\mathbf{r}_1 = \bar{\mathbf{y}}$. $\mathcal{I}$ is the index set containing columns of the sensing matrix, $\bar{\boldsymbol{\Psi}}$, identified using OMP and is initialized as the null set. For each iteration, the maximum correlating column is calculated in Step 3 and included in the index set in Step 4. The best estimate of the unknown g vector in the ith iteration is then calculated in Step 5 by projecting $\bar{\mathbf{y}}$ onto the columns of $\bar{\boldsymbol{\Psi}}$. Note that the solution is based on the least squares

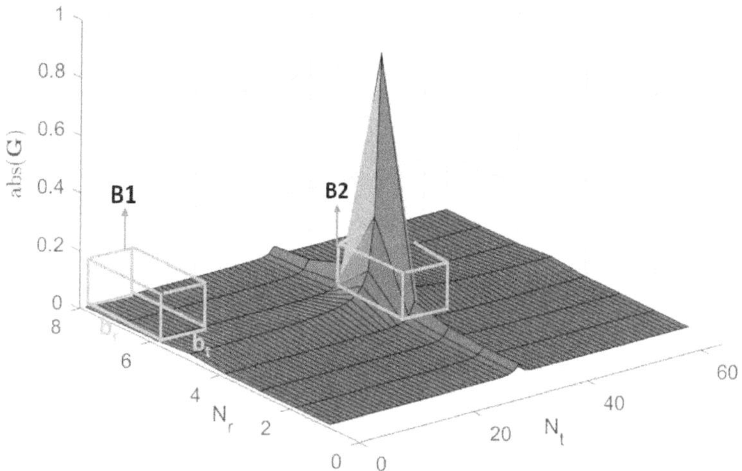

Figure 5.1: Illustration of selecting entries from a block in GBOMP

approximation. This ensures that the updated residue (which is basically the estimation error) in Step 7 is orthogonal to the columns of $\bar{\bar{\Psi}}$. The procedure is repeated until the mentioned stopping criteria is met. There are many ways to stop the OMP algorithm (Aditi *et al.*, 2020). In our work, we appropriately select the threshold τ^{OMP} to indicate the convergence of the residue signal and stop the OMP algorithm either based on τ^{OMP} or when the maximum number of iterations are reached. Then, the estimate of $\mathbf{g}$, $\hat{\mathbf{g}}$ for the identified index locations in $\mathcal{I}$ is calculated in Step 7. Other entries of $\hat{\mathbf{g}}$ are filled with 0.

5.2.2 GBOMP algorithm

Recall the block-sparse nature of the beamspace mmWave channel explained in Section 2.4 of Chapter 2. The same is shown in Figure 5.1 in which the signal energy is concentrated only within a cluster/block of bins close to the spectral frequencies. GBOMP is a modified version of OMP and exploits the block sparse nature of mmWave channels.

As explained in Algorithm 1, OMP tries to find the energy of the maximum correlating column in Step 3 and the corresponding channel gain estimate (weight vector value) at that column location. That is, OMP uses the one-to-one mapping between the entries of g with the corresponding columns of $\bar{\Psi}$. GBOMP uses a redefined metric which is the sum of the correlation energies within a series of columns of the sensing matrix. The columns are picked carefully such that the corresponding entries of g when mapped to G_i, fall within a contiguous block of bins as shown in Figure 5.1. Block size, $b_r \times b_t$, is a user-specified input parameter for GBOMP which specifies the number of bins to be grouped along the rows and the columns of the channel matrix. For example, the indices specified by block B2 in Figure 5.1 compute the metric based on the significant channel path and its leakage components. The computed metric, in this case, will be very much higher and distinctive when compared with the other metrics calculated for different block locations. GBOMP exhaustively searches for the maximum metric by considering all the block locations, including the overlapping blocks. Once the best block is identified, all the corresponding unique columns of $\bar{\Psi}$ are updated in the index set, similar to Step 4 of Algorithm 1. All the other steps for GBOMP are the same as in Algorithm 1. The detailed steps for the implementation of the GBOMP algorithm, recovery guarantees, and complexity analysis are given in (Manoj and Kannu, 2018). We have implemented GBOMP based UE algorithm for CD and evaluated the performance in Chapter 4.

5.3 COMPLEXITY ANALYSIS

Table 5.1: Computation complexity of OMP based mmWave channel estimation method with different training beams

Complexity	CBS	BC	MUBB	RBF
Training using Finer Beams, $L = N_t N_r N_B$				
# Multiplications	$i_{max}LN_S$	—	$i_{max}LN_S$	$i_{max}LN_S$
# Additions	$i_{max}LN_S$	—	$i_{max}LMN_S$	$2i_{max}LMN_S$
Training using widened beams, $L = \frac{N_t N_r}{\alpha\beta} N_B$				
# Multiplications	—	$i_{max}LN_S$	$i_{max}LN_S$	$i_{max}LN_S$
# Additions	—	$Li_{max}LN_S$	$i_{max}LMN_S$	$2i_{max}LMN_S$

In this section, we analyse the complexity of the channel estimation using OMP algorithm. As explained in Section 4.7, the overhead involved can be divided into training overhead, algorithm complexity and storage complexity.

The training overhead is equal to MN_S and depends on the number of symbols transmitted. Here M is the number of transmit-receive beam pairs and N_S is the sequence length. Algorithm complexity for channel estimation depends on the number of runs of OMP algorithm and the complexity involved in each of its execution. For fair comparison of all the schemes, we neglect the residue condition for termination in Algorithm 1 and assume that the OMP algorithm run for i_{max} iterations. For each ith iteration, algorithm will then correlate with all columns of $\bar{\Psi}$ except the columns detected in the preceding $i - 1$ iterations. Table 4.2 gives the complexity for one run of step 3 of OMP algorithm. Using the same procedure, it is easy to compute the complexity of step 5 and step 7. This involves a total of iN_S multiplications and $(i + 1)MN_S - 2$ complex additions. For example, the number of complex multiplications and complex additions required for MUBB method for i^{th} iteration will be $(L+1)(N_S+1) - i$ and $(L-i)(MN_S - 1) - 2$ respectively. This can be easily extended to calculate the computation complexity of channel estimation by taking cumulative sum of the complexity values. The approximate results by considering only the dominant terms are summarised in Table 5.1. The computation complexity for channel estimation using GBOMP algorithm can also be calculated similarly.

5.4 METRICS FOR CHANNEL ESTIMATION

In this section, we define the metrics used for comparing the performance of channel estimation algorithms. We quantify the estimation error in terms of Normalised Mean Squared Error (NMSE), defined as,

$$\text{NMSE} = \mathbb{E}\left(\frac{||\mathbf{g} - \hat{\mathbf{g}}||^2}{||\mathbf{g}||^2}\right) \tag{5.4}$$

NMSE is unitless and is plotted in a dB scale.

The beamforming vectors calculated based on the estimated channel is then used susequently for communication. Average beamforming gain (γ) and Asymptotic Spectral Efficiency (ASE) are particularly important during the data transfer phase and are defined as below.

$$\gamma = \mathbb{E}\left(\frac{1}{N_B}\sum_{i=1}^{N_B} |\hat{\mathbf{u}}_\mathbf{i}^H \mathbf{H}_i \hat{\mathbf{v}}_\mathbf{i}|^2\right) \tag{5.5}$$

Here $\hat{\mathbf{u}}_\mathbf{i}$ and $\hat{\mathbf{v}}_\mathbf{i}$ are the left and right singular vectors corresponding to the maximum singular value of the channel estimate $\hat{\mathbf{H}}_i$ calculated from $\hat{\mathbf{G}}_\mathbf{i}$. γ only considers the goodness of the channel estimate and does not take into account the training duration.

$$\text{ASE} = \left(1 - \frac{M}{T}\right)\mathbb{E}\left(\frac{1}{N_B}\sum_{i=1}^{N_B}\log_2\left(1 + \frac{|\hat{\mathbf{u}}_\mathbf{i}^H\mathbf{H}_i\hat{\mathbf{v}}_\mathbf{i}|^2}{\sigma^2}\right)\right) \tag{5.6}$$

$M = \frac{PQ}{N_{rf}}$ is the total number of beamforming vector pairs used and governs the training duration. T is the coherence time of the mmWave channel in terms of the number of symbols. Hence, $\frac{M}{T}$ denotes the fraction of time devoted for training purpose. σ^2 is the variance of the additive noise. Thus ASE depends on both training duration and beamforming gain.

5.5   SIMULATION RESULTS

In this section, we study the detailed performance of channel estimation problem with different training schemes. Since the channel estimation phase happens after the CD step, UE would have been linked with a smaller subset of BSs after CD, even if there are a large number of BSs in the mmWave network. Hence, we consider a network of 4 BSs and assume all the BSs as active. The antenna set-up, number of RF chains, and the mmWave channels are generated in the same way as discussed in Section 3.5.1. Assuming an average of 3 paths per BS, we fix the maximum number of loops for OMP-based implementation as, $i_{max} = 12$. We fix the block size for GBOMP algorithm as $b = 2 \times 2$. Hence, the maximum number of iterations for GBOMP is fixed as 3 for a fair comparison with OMP, so that both OMP and GBOMP detect 12 entries.

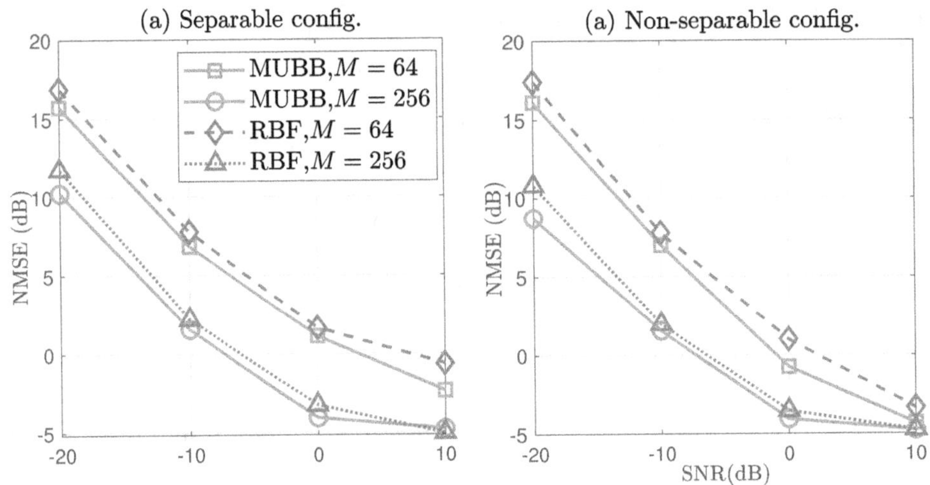

Figure 5.2: NMSE vs SNR using OMP algorithm with separable and non-separable antenna configurations

5.5.1 NMSE vs SNR

The variation of the channel estimation error with SNR using OMP algorithm is plotted in Figure 5.2. We observe that the NMSE decreases with SNR for all the schemes. NMSE for MUBB scheme is lesser than the RBF scheme for both separable and non-separable antenna configurations because of the lower mutual coherence of the sensing matrix. Further, a higher M indicates a larger training duration and hence a lower NMSE value. Thus $M = 256$ outperforms $M = 64$ for all the training schemes.

In Figure 5.3, NMSE variation with respect to SNR is shown for training schemes using widened beams, discussed in Chapter 4. As explained in Section 4.3, the compressive sensing model with the widened beams recovers the coarser lower resolution beamspace matrix. Hence, the estimated channel will also be an approximation of this lower-dimension channel. Thus, NMSE, in this case, is calculated by replacing the original channel with the lower dimension beamspace channel in (5.4). We see that MUBB$^{(w)}$

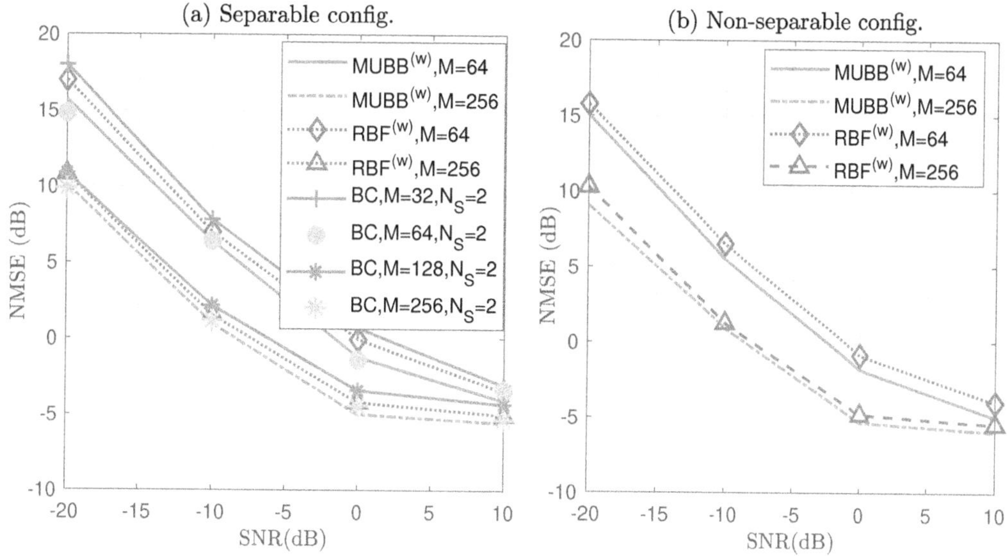

Figure 5.3: NMSE vs SNR using OMP algorithm using widened beams. $N_S = 1$ for MUBB and RBF schemes.

outperforms RBF$^{(w)}$ scheme for both separable and non-separable configuration. As explained in Chapter 3, BC scheme uses the same training vectors for all BSs; UE cannot estimate the channel from multiple BSs unless a synchronization sequence specific to each BS is transmitted. For comparison, we set the synchronization sequences as MUB vectors of length 2 for the BC method. From Figure 5.3, we observe that the BC scheme with $M = 256, N_S = 2$ shows almost similar NMSE variation when compared with MUBB$^{(w)}$ and RBF$^{(w)}$ methods for $M = 256$. In account of the transmit sequence, to maintain the same total number of symbols transmitted ($MN_S = 256$) as MUBB$^{(w)}$ and RBF$^{(w)}$ methods, M for BC needs to be reduced to half, ie, $M = 128$. We observe from Figure 5.3 that in terms of the schemes with the same training duration MN_S, MUBB$^{(w)}$ outperforms both RBF and BC methods for both separable and non-separable configurations. Similar results are observed when M is reduced to 64.

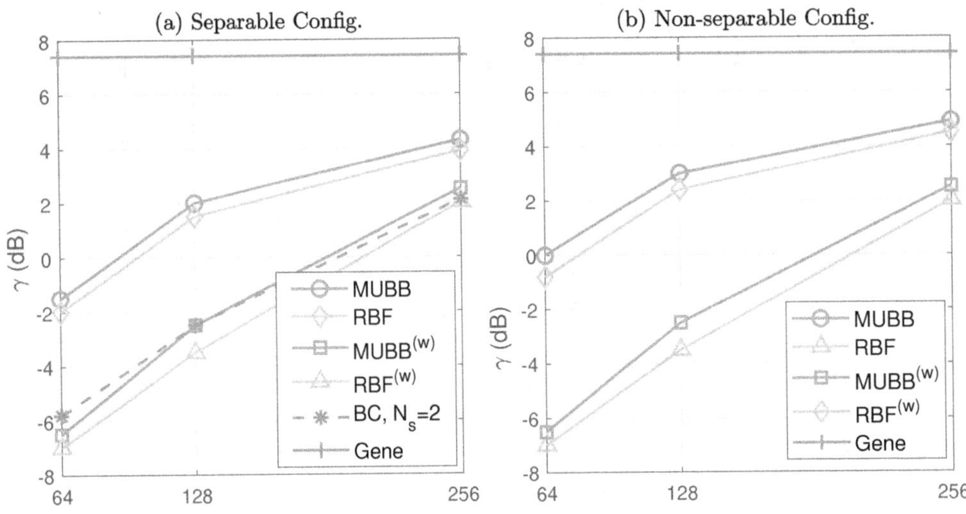

Figure 5.4: Beamforming gain vs M using OMP algorithm

5.5.2 Beamforming gain vs M

Inverse DFT operation on the estimated beamspace channel gives the millimeter wave channel estimate. For training schemes using widened beams, first $\hat{g}$ needs to be calculated from $\hat{g}^{(w)}$ using the transformation given in (5.3). UE then feeds back this information to the BS. Maximum beamforming gain can then be achieved by using left and right singular vectors of the estimate as the transmit and receive beamforming vectors.

We compute the average of this maximum beamforming gains as defined in (5.5) and plot in Figure 5.4. SNR is fixed as $-5dB$. We observe that γ decreases with M for all the schemes as the sensing matrix becomes wider and wider. This increases the mutual coherence of $\bar{\Psi}$ and hence adversely affects the recovery performance of OMP algorithm. The figure indicates the superior performance of MUBB method over the training schemes for both separable and non-separable configurations. Further, owing to a sensing matrix with lower mutual coherence, training schemes using a non-separable antenna configuration outperform its separable counterpart for all M values. We also notice that the schemes without widening offer better beamforming gain than the schemes with widened beams for all M values. Channel estimation using coarser beams senses the lower dimensional beamspace channel. The transformation to full dimension channel introduces a lot of error in the estimate, and the alignment of the singular vectors calculated from the estimate can be far different from the vectors of the original channel. This results in a poor beamforming gain for schemes using coarser beams. $MUBB$ and RBF methods, on the other hand, estimate the full resolution channel and hence reveals more accurate SVD training vectors. BC scheme shows slightly better performance when compared with MUBB$^{(w)}$ and RBF$^{(w)}$ at $M = 64$ but with twice the number of symbols transmitted as explained in Section 5.5.1.

5.5.3 ASE vs M

ASE is defined in (5.6). We fix $T = 1000$ for simulations. The scaling factor $(1 - \frac{M}{T})$ denotes the fraction of time available for data transfer and hence decreases with an increase in the training duration M. The beamforming gain given by $|\hat{\mathbf{u}}_i^H \mathbf{H}_i \hat{\mathbf{v}}_i|^2$ increases with M as the channel estimate becomes better. The dependence of ASE on M relies on the values of both these terms. Figure 5.5 shows the variation of ASE of different training schemes with M values. The performance trend is similar to the beamforming gain plot in Figure 5.4.

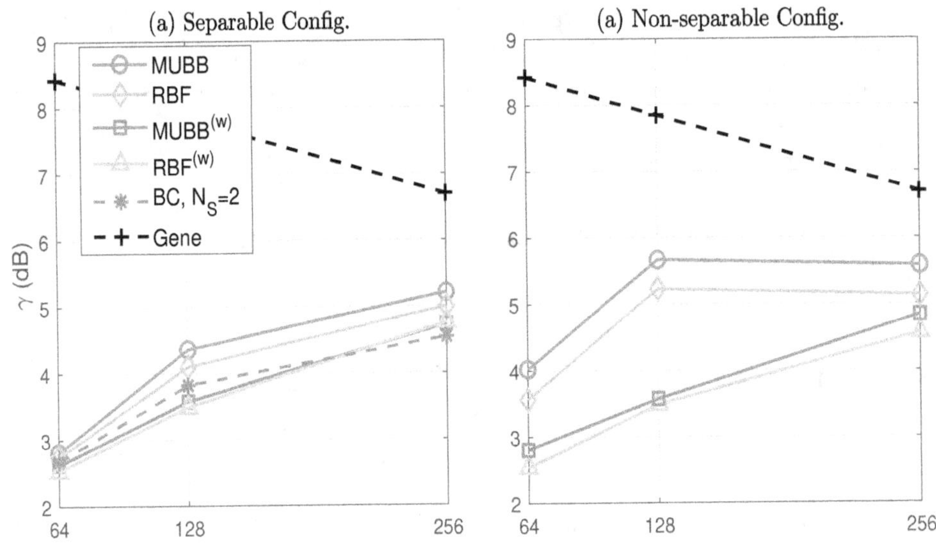

Figure 5.5: ASE vs M using OMP algorithm, $SNR = -5dB$

5.5.4 Performance comparison with ULAs.

In this section, we show the performance when linear arrays are used at the BSs and UE in Figure 5.6. The CBS scheme with $M = 64$ and $N_S = 2$ outperforms the MUBB and RBF methods with $MN_S = 64$ because of the use of transmit sequence. However, when the BC scheme is implemented to meet $MN_S = 64$, both $\mathbb{P}_D$ and γ deteriorate because of the presence of coarse beams. In fact, MUBB and RBF methods with $MN_S = 32$ outperform the same for $SNR \geq -3dB$.

5.5.5 Results with GBOMP algorithm

In Figure 5.7(a) and (b), we study the error and the beamforming gain performances of different training schemes with GBOMP algorithm for separable antenna configuration. First, we notice that the performance of GBOMP algorithm is very much comparable

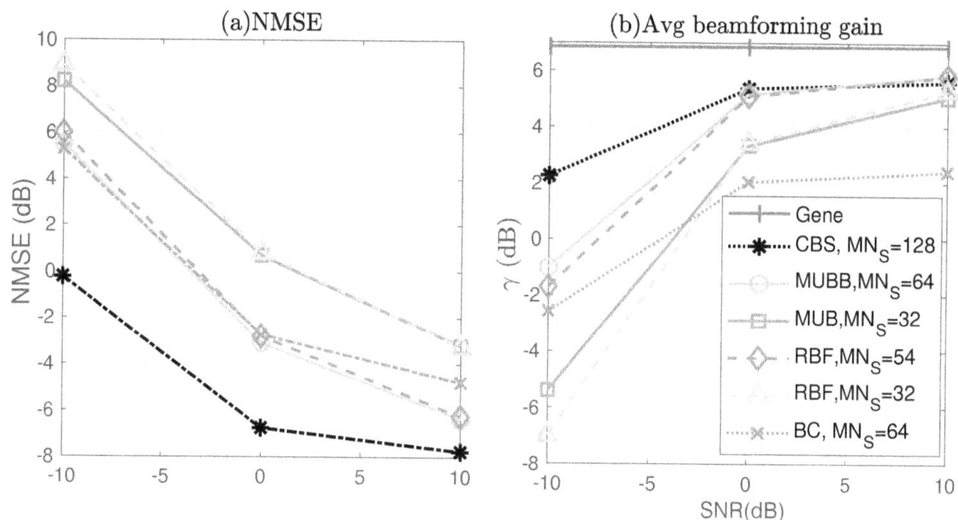

Figure 5.6: NMSE and Beamforming gain performance using ULA set up.

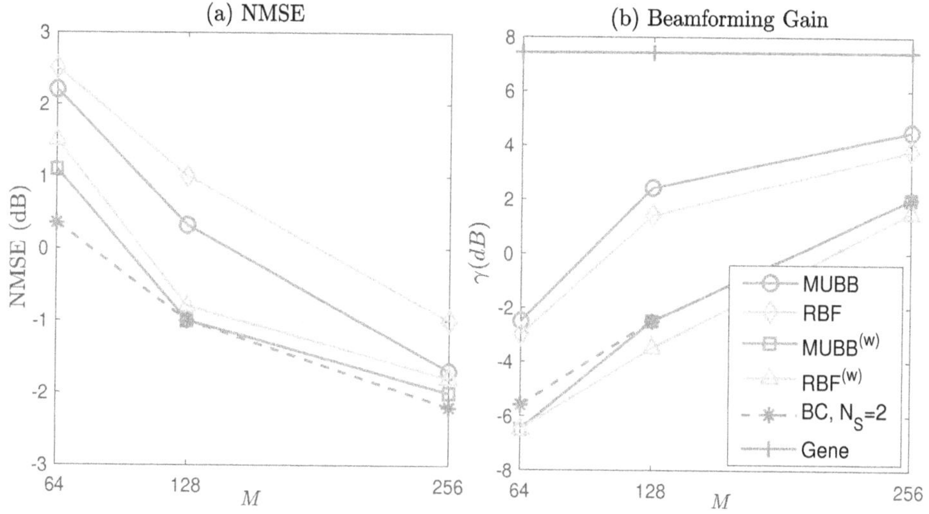

Figure 5.7: NMSE and Beamforming gain performance with GBOMP algorithm,SNR=-5dB

with that of the OMP algorithm shown in Figure 5.2, Figure 5.3 and Figure 5.4. We also observe the superior performance of MUB-based schemes for both coarser and finer beam-based methods. The NMSE and beamforming gain values show the same trend as that obtained using the OMP algorithm, thus confirming the applicability of MUBB based training scheme for channel estimation with GBOMP algorithm.

5.6 SUMMARY

In this chapter, we applied the MUB-based training beamforming vectors to solve the channel estimation problem in mmWave networks with multiple RF chains without any feedback from the UE during the training phase. Starting from the compressive sensing model developed for the cell discovery work, we formulated the channel estimation problem and discussed how to use any sparse recovery algorithm for channel estimation. For comparison purposes, we focused on two greedy algorithms, namely, OMP and GBOMP algorithms, and briefly explained both with specific emphasis on the mmWave channel estimation problem. We also incorporated the training schemes using coarser beams for faster channel estimation. Finally, we studied the performance of all the MUBB, RBF, and BC training schemes with practical mmWave channels generated using NYUSIM simulator, and verified the superior performance of MUB based training scheme in terms of Normalised Mean Squared Error, Beamforming gain, and Asymptotic Spectral Efficiency. The results were established with both OMP and GBOMP receiver algorithms and for both separable and non-separable antenna configurations.